The St. Francis Camino

A Spiritual Walking Pilgrimage from Assisi to Rome

Bret Thoman, OFS

FOREWORD

By Mons. Paolo Giulietti
Archbishop of Lucca

PILGRIMAGE: A DYNAMIC FOR CHANGE

What distinguishes pilgrimages from other methods of traveling? Not its means of motion, as trekkers also go on foot; not interest in nature or art, which many forms of tourism have as a concern; not its search for silence and solitude, attainable in any monastery; not its frugality or means of saving money, also characteristic of the *routard* [the French version of the *Hitch-hiker's Guide to Europe*]. Most likely it is the presence of an expectation regarding the goal of the experience, which always implies the prospect of change. One becomes a pilgrim – starting from any kind of motivation - because one desires to change.

The film, *The Way,* starring Emilio Estevez and Martin Sheen, captures this dynamic well: all the protagonists — each with their motivations and beliefs — are ultimately driven by the expectation of change, and in the end, each character ends up transformed, even if perhaps in unexpected ways. The profound desire to experience a transforming experience (similar to a conversion, "*meta-noia*") — constitutes the *raison d'etre* of the pilgrimage.

On the other hand, the sanctuary — the goal of the Camino — is a place that possesses, by virtue of some manifestation of the divine, particular qualities and properties in relation to some aspect of life that one desires to change: an illness to be healed, a sin to be expiated, a relationship to be restored, a circumstance to be overcome, a vow to be undone. It is not a given that exactly what one desires will take place, but something must and can take place!

The Dynamics of Change: Seven Essential "Ingredients"

So how does change come about on pilgrimage? What are the dynamics through which the desire for transformation reaches fulfillment? As the pilgrimage diaries of yesterday and today testify, it consists of processes that involve all the dimensions of the person: the body, spirit and soul. Grace certainly acts within these dynamics to produce the spiritual fruits of conversion, but it also deals with phenomena exquisitely anthropological, and not necessarily limited to Christian pilgrimage.

The First Dynamic is Detachment

In beginning the journey, one must leave everyday life in order to enter a new relationship with space and time; in this, one assumes a different identity — that of a pilgrim. There exist — both yesterday and today — numerous "rituals" that mark this passage: writing one's testament, vesting oneself with particular attire and symbolic objects, bidding farewell to what one holds dear. By virtue of this distancing from everyday life, one's entire life is oriented differently and is aimed at reaching a goal. This goal is not limited to the point of arrival, rather it becomes a criterion for each choice and the organization of one's day.

And still today, setting off involves detachment from everyday things, the renunciation of objects and habits believed to be essential. Special clothing is acquired, a walking pack is chosen and donned, and a modern "pilgrim's staff," (perhaps walking poles) are brought. The pilgrim dons the symbols of the journey: a shell, a group shirt, a TAU cross, a pin …

This remains a process ritualized with wisdom, perhaps underlined with certain challenges: "Leave your tablet at home!" — or with the revival of some ancient form of investiture.

The Second Dynamic is Fatigue

Discomfort, fatigue, and uncertainty are all structural components of the pilgrimage. In the past, this was referred to as "penance" inasmuch as suffering and humiliation were embraced as means of purification and ways of combating evil inclinations and acts in order to achieve authentic inner renewal. In the case of judicial pilgrimages (those imposed by a judge) or penitential (imposed by one's confessor), this expiatory dimension acquired the utmost primary value.

Yet even today the fatigue of walking and experiencing discomfort remain important aspects of the journey. The pilgrim experiences his or her own inadequacy as well as possibilities; the surprising discovery of being able to make the journey or the bitter awareness of one's limits are both important factors of truth: one's masks fall one after the other. Reaching the goal is almost always experienced as a moment of catharsis (tears, hugs, confession) precisely because it crowns and celebrates that which fatigue has led to along the way.

As organizers, the temptation to reduce or outright eliminate fatigue and discomfort must be overcome (without turning the pilgrimage into a Calvary). Instead, it is important to share in its surprising interior resonance.

The Third Dynamic is Solitude

This is perhaps the most modern aspect of the pilgrimage. In ancient times, people rarely set out alone, as companionship was an indispensable source of support as well as the appropriate context. Consider that the fraternal pilgrimages of the seventeenth century were undertaken as solemn processions — with banners and bands playing music!

The possibility of enjoying solitary spaces and long moments of silence appears today as an essential component of the Camino. Precisely because quiet and silence are rare commodities in our hectic modern world, they are particularly sought out and appreciated as an opportunity to "return to oneself" as part of the workshop of the spiritual path. Clearly, the longer and more solitary the Camino, the more opportunities are offered for one's interiority. Silence also creates space for the goal, enhancing its motivating power and charging it with desires, images, expectations.

The Fourth Dynamic is Companionship

In the past, people walked virtually always with others. The pilgrim people lived of encounters, knowledge, and mutual support. For this reason, a common identity matured along the pilgrimage routes: "Europe was born on pilgrimage and its language is Christianity" (Goethe).

Still today pilgrimage offers the experience of a unique form of companionship united in the sharing of moments of walk or rest. It is a singular experience of humanity (and catholicity), to which non-pilgrims contribute along the way through surprising gestures or by supporting the journey through service. Thus, the constitutive need of the other emerges and the false notion of self-sufficiency collapses: others are necessary to us, as we are to others. The result is often a new trust in humanity, together with a desire to experience one's relationships differently (solidarity, intergenerationality). In the crowds and in the solemn rituals upon reaching the goal, the people of the Camino become visible and celebrate their communion together.

Yet there is also an invisible companionship that characterizes the Camino. Loved ones — both living and deceased — whom we all carry in our hearts, whose presence emerges in the surprising strength of interiority or even in conversations: the "communion of saints," as we would say, on the Camino, is a reality.

Consider, as well, that it is important not to settle for "closed" companionship. Even when one experiences the pilgrimage in a group setting, the widest relationships possible make for an important formative resource.

The Fifth Dynamic is Wonder

In the past, undertaking a pilgrimage was the journey of a lifetime for many: it was an opportunity to get to know new places and cultures, to admire landscapes, cities, and large cathedrals. The ancient travel narratives underscore the pleasure of discovery (even gastronomic!) and the pilgrim's wonder before the masterpieces of architecture and art within the sanctuaries.

Yet today one is still struck by many things on Camino: a renewed experience of creation; the keen perception of the territory that arises only from traversing it on foot; the opportunity of enjoying art and vestiges of the past dotting the route. One has time to "gaze" on the world and not just "see" it passing by through the window of a car or tour bus. The pilgrim learns to stop, and in this, he/she is no longer a "consumer", but a contemplative. He/she recognizes and appreciates the little, but magnificent, things: the fact that they are there is not taken for granted, but they fill with gratitude and wonder.

A wise guide will not fail to emphasize, along the way, what is worth stopping for. And this arouses awareness, appreciation and reflection.

The Sixth Dynamic is Tradition

The pilgrim walks in the wake of a tradition that can be new: the friend who recounts something on Facebook that inspires; or ancient: the pilgrim, Egeria, who transmits the charm of the Holy Land in her diary of sixteen centuries ago. A "true" way of pilgrimage, thus, leads others to retrace the footsteps of those who have already traveled the same path — whose tracks appear not only in diaries, but in the setting of the territory, in the manifestations of art, in the dissemination of symbols.

This is not a question of "engaging in archeology", but of letting ourselves be "led" in a deeper sense — the route, but also its meanings and wonder. We do not create this for ourselves; rather we receive it from others. Medieval pilgrims knew this well, as they did not have maps or road signs; instead, they were forced to continually refer to the writings of someone who had gone before or to adhere to the directions of local inhabitants.

Many pilgrims become protagonists of this dynamic when, having completed the Camino, they themselves become narrators. It's almost as if they are striving, in writing, for the fulfillment of the experience: to be completely fulfilled, [the Camino] requires verbalization and communication. Pen and paper have not lost their charm, even if most people nowadays record their experiences on the trail on a tablet or post them directly online complete with photos of the route. Thus, the Camino is narrated and handed down, as, by virtue of recounting, one becomes both promoter and guide of the experience.

The Seventh Dynamic is Prayer

From the "Song of Ascents" of the psalmist to the esicastic practices of the Russian Pilgrim, prayer belongs structurally to the Camino and reaches its climax in the rituals celebrated within the holy places — especially at departure and upon arrival.

Today this is no longer so obvious, especially for the many who claim to approach the experience out of curiosity, who are trying something fashionable, or who are looking for a low-cost holiday. On pilgrimage, however, transcendence slips in almost without noticing. Ultimately, when one abandons everyday life, sets out toward a goal, and embraces fatigue, he/she adopts the logic of transcendence. Along the road, thus, the pilgrim encounters people and occasions imbued with the essence of the divine that touch the heart. This does not always take place during outward or formal prayer: sometimes it is more of a confused yearning toward the Mystery, which needs to be interpreted and oriented.

On pilgrimage there is no lack of opportunities for moments of prayer, which almost always find an unexpected inner response. The beauty of creation and art certainly help. What matters most, however, is the emergence of sentiments and perceptions, perhaps unfamiliar, which lead toward relationship with the Mystery that has drawn near. The change that was perhaps sought confusedly can finally be embraced as a gift from the One who makes all things new.

INTRODUCTION TO THE "ST. FRANCIS CAMINO"

The "*Via di Francesco*" and what I refer to as the "St. Francis Camino" is the result of a number of initiatives that came together over time.

One of the first Franciscan walking trails in central Italy was "*Il Sentiero Francescano della Pace*" (The Franciscan Peace Path). Conceived in the late 1990s as a walking trail from Assisi to Gubbio by the municipalities of Gubbio, Valfabbrica and Assisi, it received funding for the Jubilee preparations of 2000.

Another trail from the early 2000s was spearheaded in Rieti by Diego di Paolo. The trail was called the "*Cammino di Francesco*" (The Camino of Francis) and sought to connect the four Franciscan sanctuaries in the environs of Rieti: Poggio Bustone, La Foresta, Fonte Colombo, and Greccio. It was realized in 2003 by the administrative Province of Rieti with the collaboration of the OFM Franciscan friars of Lazio. In the beginning, wooden signposts were used to mark the trail.

Also in the early years was a loosely organized trail from Laverna (in Tuscany) to Assisi that went by different names. Some called it the "Sentiero Francescano" (Franciscan Trail) while others referred to it as the "Sentiero di Francesco" (Trail of Francis).

Next, Angela Seracchioli, an Italian mountain enthusiast and true trailblazer, walked from Assisi to Greccio inventing the trail as she went along with the mere idea of walking where St. Francis walked. Along the way, she took notes, later unintentionally crossed paths with a book publisher, and the result was her pioneering guidebook, "*Di qui passò Francesco*" (*On the Road with Saint Francis*) published by Terre di Mezzo.

Then there was Kees Roodenburg, a hiking aficionado from the

Netherlands with plenty of experience on the St. James Camino in Spain. He heard about the Franciscan trails in central Italy, walked one, and also wrote a guidebook. Written in his native Dutch, it was translated into German and published with the title, *Franziskusweg*. Thereafter, the Italian countryside began teeming with pilgrims from the Germanic countries eager for an alternative to the crowded Spanish St. James Camino.

With the success and publicity of these various initiatives, a larger project was conceived: a Santiago-like Camino trail in Italy traversing multiple regions in the footsteps and land of St. Francis and inspired by his spirituality. Such an idea was mostly foreign to Italians as the culture of Camino was virtually non-existent in Italy at the time. But with this endeavor, larger players got involved.

The administrative region of Umbria played a lead role with support from Lazio as well as the Vatican. Additionally there was the Province of Rieti (under the leadership of Diego Di Paolo), together with the Franciscans of Lazio. The Basilica of St. Francis in Assisi and the Umbrian conference of bishops also played a role, as did numerous municipalities throughout Umbria that would be along the route. (It should be noted that Tuscany and other regions were invited to participate, but initially declined.)

All these individuals recognized that walking in the same land where the *Poverello* himself walked — in the very places connected to his life and preaching — would be an extraordinary and unparalleled Franciscan journey. At the same time, Rome, the Eternal City, has always been an important destination for pilgrims devoted to St. Peter, so it only made sense that the trail, as all "roads," would lead to Rome.

The Camino was designed to be self-guided for pilgrims on foot, bicycle or even horseback. A comprehensive website was launched, and maps were created. Yellow and blue metal signposts were cemented along the trail and paint stripes were marked on trees and rocks. Hotels, agritourisms, and B&Bs put their names on the list for accommodations, while GPX tracks were created and guidebooks improved. Credentials and Testimonium certificates were printed.

In the beginning, the Camino was divided into various sections with different names. There was the northern, Umbrian-managed "*Via Francigena di San Francesco*" (The Via Francigena of St. Francis) which began at the border of Umbria and Tuscany, went southward through Assisi, and ended at the border with Lazio. There, Rieti's "*Cammino di Francesco*" picked up and offered pilgrims the possibility of staying a few extra days to walk the existing trails connecting the four Franciscan sanctuaries. Finally, the southern "*Via di Roma*" ("Way of Rome") went from Rieti all the way to Rome where it terminated at St. Peter's Basilica in the Vatican.

The Camino trail was created by frequently piggybacking on existing trails. Often, CAI hiking footpaths (Club Alpino Italiano) — marked with red and white stripes with numbers that corresponded to trails on maps — were used, while in other places, the Camino followed other local spiritual trails (such as the "*Sentiero Francescano della pace*" trail between Assisi and Gubbio). When dirt trails were not possible, the organizers utilized paved secondary or dirt roads.

Inaugurated in 2007, the project was well-received, and the culture of the Camino was on its way to being established in Italy.

As an interesting linguistic historical note, the naming of the trail, "*Cammino di Francesco*" is the first case in the Italian language in which the Italian word "*Cammino*" was used in the same way as the Spanish word, "*Camino*"; that is, a sustained, spiritual walking journey on foot. Prior to this introduction, the word, *Cammino*, in Italian meant simply "path" or "pathway." Instead, words like "*sentiero*" (trail), "*via*" (way), "*escursione*" (excursion) or the English word, trekking, were used, rather forcedly, to indicate the longer camino-like experience, though they never totally captured the true meaning of the word. (Here I should add that I use the Spanish spelling, Camino, for my English usage of the word, recognizing that *camino* in Italian means "fireplace".)

Umbria was ultimately forced to change the name of their section of the trail, *Via Francigena di San Francesco*, after gripes began to come in from northern European that the actual Via Francigena was a medieval Camino that began in Canterbury, England, passed through France and Switzerland before arriving in Italy, and had nothing to do with St. Francis or Umbria. Thus, the Umbrians changed its name to the *Via di Francesco* (The Way of Francis), which remains the official name today. (By the way, Umbria would have preferred to utilize the name, "*Cammino di Francesco*," but it was already taken by Lazio, and they were unable to reach an agreement on sharing the name.

Over time, administrators in Tuscany realized the success of the trail and decided they wanted to get involved. Laverna, where St. Francis received the stigmata, thus has become an important site of the Camino, and Florence became a possible point of departure. In fact, Sandy Brown, in his English guidebook *The Way of Francis*, begins in Florence and continues to Rome over the course of thirty days. Though the Camino in Tuscany initially followed mostly red and white CAI markings, there has been a concerted effort recently to go over to the standardized blue and yellow markings.

And it is this network of trails — that began at different times for diverse reasons – that is generally referred to in Italian now as the *Via di Francesco*, and what I refer to as the "St. Francis Camino."

Further, it should be noted that the official Camino has been modified over the years for various reasons: a new highway cut through the trail, a landowner complained about people traipsing through his fields, severe weather eroded away a trail, or alternative stages were added. When changes were made, the original signposts were left in their original places while new ones were added. The result is a sometimes-confusing hodgepodge of way markings, signposts, and maps.

Though it may all seem confusing, the various entities involved have been working together and striving to create a unified Camino. The St. Francis Camino route can be fairly easily navigated with a little bit of planning and preparation. The entire route is marked with yellow and blue markings and metal signs, and GPX tracks are available. With a guidebook, GPX tracks, and by following the yellow/blue markings along the trail, navigation is assured.

Indeed, the trend along the St. Francis Camino continues to be upward. According to data from the Assisi pilgrimage office, *Statio peregrinorum*, over 4,000 people walked all or portions of the trail in Umbria in 2019. While the majority of Camino walkers are Italians, a sizeable number are coming from Germany, France, the United States, Austria, the Netherlands, and even Brazil. And the numbers continue to increase by about ten percent every year.

AUTHOR'S PREFACE

The St. Francis Camino from Assisi to Rome is an extraordinary experience, and I remember quite vividly the sensation I had upon arriving in St. Peter's Basilica to claim my *Testimonium* completion certificate. Though I had been to Rome countless times, I will never forget the elation and sense of accomplishment I felt arriving in the Eternal City on foot. I will confess, too, some pride and superiority at having arrived not by bus or car, but the way pilgrims once travelled in the past.

And though the climax of arrival was particularly poignant, I also recall moments of exuberance on the trail. Just before Cantalice, in one instance, I recall coming around a bend on a mountain trail to discover the medieval hill town draped before me almost like a magnificent tapestry hanging in a museum. I called a friend of mine that evening and told him I felt like I was falling in love.

I have walked the entirety of the Camino, in bits and pieces, a total of about three times. Yet, I have walked some stages many more times while accompanying pilgrims.

Since then, I have learned much about the trail. Yet, and perhaps more importantly, I have come to learn about how people respond to it. Most pilgrims are knowledgeable and arrive well-trained and prepared for the Camino. However, some are not.

Back home in coastal Florida or the flatlands of the American Midwest, they were easily able to speed-walk twelve miles (20 kilometers) for training. Yet when they arrive in Italy and look up at the mean Apennine peaks, they quickly understand why elevation changes are emphasized in each day's route description.

This book is the result of what I have learned about the St. Francis

Camino. It is not intended to be a detailed step-by-step guidebook. The best option in English for such a book is *The Way of Francis* by Sandy Brown, which I strongly recommend. This book, instead, focuses more on the spiritual aspect of the pilgrimage. As such, I drew on my knowledge of the life of St. Francis from my formation as a Third Order Franciscan in addition to research for my books on St. Francis and Clare.

Each stage includes daily distances, cumulative altitude gains and losses, surface type, duration (assuming a very moderate pace of three kilometers per hour), and level of difficulty. Distances are listed with metric system.

I rated each stage with one of the following levels of difficulty: Easy, Moderate, Difficult, Very Difficult, Experts Only. Certainly, this is subjective and what one person considers difficult could be easy to another. At any rate, after having walked the Camino a few days, you will be able to use the rating system to compare one day's level to another. Next, I include a brief description of the stage followed by notes pertaining to safety, clarification, reminders, or special places not to be missed.

Next is the textual description of the route. To reiterate, this book does not describe the route in an overly detailed, step-by-step format (*The Way of Francis* guidebook does that). For navigation, there are blue and yellow signposts and paint markings along the way, as well as GPX tracks that can be easily installed on a smartphone or a portable GPS device. (See section on GPX tracks below.)

After the textual description, I list the Franciscan sites along the route followed by other places of interest not necessarily connected to the life of St. Francis, but significant places to be aware of. Lastly, I include an aerial online map of the trail as well as an elevation profile.

It is my hope that this guidebook will be a blessing to you as you prepare for the St. Francis Camino.

PREPARATION

PACKING

Pilgrims frequently lament bringing too much stuff. Packing wisely is strongly recommended.

Here is a list of essential items you should bring on your Camino:

- <u>Hiking boots or shoes</u>: This may be your most important purchase, as it is imperative to have a good, well-fitting, broken-in pair of hiking shoes or boots. Some participants prefer boots for ankle support and protection in the mountains, while others like hiking shoes (Merrell is a popular brand) or trail runners. In any case, you want footwear that is lightweight with a cushioned sole. It should fit well and be broken in before departure. Another important consideration is keeping your feet dry; therefore, we strongly recommend waterproof or water-resistant footwear. Not only are the inner linings of wet boots difficult to dry after a downpour, walking for long stretches in wet shoes can damage the skin.

- <u>Hiking pack:</u> If you are planning on carrying all your gear, you should bring a hiking pack of at a very minimum of 60 liters (preferably larger). If you will be using daily luggage transport service, you can bring a smaller day pack. In either case, the pack should be waterproof, or else have a rain protective liner.

- <u>Hiking Wear:</u> Make sure your garments are designed for hiking or running. They should be lightweight, of poly material, and quick-dry. Do not bring cotton material which is heavy when wet (or sweaty) and takes a long time to dry; denim is worse and takes even longer to dry. We recommend bringing three sets of each garment: one set will be worn during the day, one pair is to change into after hiking, and one will be drying after being washed the previous day.

- <u>Shorts or pants</u>: Shorts are good for warmer walking, though in late Fall or early Spring, we recommend bringing pants with removable legs option to convert into shorts.

- <u>Shirts:</u> You should bring some short sleeve running shirts; on warm days they're the only shirt you will need. When it's cooler you'll want some long-sleeve shirts, as well. You can use the long sleeves as a base layer for cold or wet days.

- <u>Socks/Sock liners</u>: We recommend bringing hiking socks which have reinforced padding in areas of the foot prone to blistering. Some participants bring sock liners which help prevent blisters by creating a slick surface between the foot and the sock: silk is best, but there are less expensive options.

- <u>Toiletries</u>: toothbrush/toothpaste, deodorant, soap, shampoo, medicines, etc.

- <u>Clothes pins and clothesline</u>: As laundry facilities are limited on the trail, you may want to bring travel clotheslines to do some laundry in hotel sinks. Plan on around two- to three-meter clothesline and four to six clothespins for hanging up laundry to dry.

- <u>Walking Poles</u>: Though Americans are less accustomed to hiking with walking sticks, they are standard accessories for most Europeans. Experts say poles redistribute up to 30% of energy from your legs to your upper body giving you more endurance. If you bring them from home, make sure they go in your checked suitcase, as they may not be permitted as carry-on items.

- <u>Evening clothes</u>: After each day's hike you'll want to have something comfortable to wear and everyone has their own preference. Make sure you bring a separate comfortable pair of non-hiking shoes like Crocs or sandals.

If you'll be using daily luggage transfer services, you should bring with you the following supplies in your day pack:

- <u>A guidebook</u>: a good guidebook is essential, as it will offer step-by-step information on each day's hike.

- <u>Cell phone or GPS unit</u>: An operable smart phone is practically a standard accessory nowadays. It is handy for GPX tracks, emergency calls (if necessary), photography, and Wi-Fi. Consider getting a good international plan with data roaming, as it may come in handy along the trail. Otherwise, keep your data turned off, or in Airplane Mode, while away from Wi-Fi, as unexpected international roaming charges may await you with your next bill. If you don't use a smart phone, consider bringing an economical handheld GPS unit to follow the trail (see below for information on GPX tracks).

- <u>Rain jacket or poncho</u>: you can either bring a nicer hiking jacket (with Gore-Tex and sealed seams), or a more economical compact poncho.

- <u>Fleece sweatshirt</u>: On cool mornings, you should begin by layering with a fleece sweatshirt; it can be removed when you warm up and put into your day pack.

- <u>Sun/rain hat</u>: You will want a hat with a wide brim to protect your face, ears and neck from sun exposure in addition to rain. You may wish to bring sunglasses, as well as sun block cream.

- <u>Water bladder or bottle</u>: It is essential to carry water each day. Many participants use water bladders, like Camelbak, which makes rehydrating easy through a tube. While there are some fountains along the way, they are not always accessible, or potable. Therefore, you should plan to carry your water with you before setting out (tap water in hotels is potable). During the summer, or hot days, you should set out with no less than 4 liters (one gallon) of water.

- <u>Identification</u>: Legally, you are required to carry some form of identification on your person at all times; it should be your passport, though it can be your state- or national-issued driver's license. It should go in a plastic or waterproof bag in case of rain infiltration. You might also want to keep your official Camino Pilgrim's Passport in the plastic bag, too.

- <u>Blister kit</u>: The onset of blisters will necessitate prompt attention since few things can affect a Camino worse than blistered feet. It is imperative that "hot spots" be addressed before they become full-on blisters. There are many good kits on the market.

- <u>Toilet tissue</u>: You'll want to have some TP with you on the trail in case you need to make an unscheduled trip to the (natural) restroom facilities located all alongside the trail.

- <u>ATM card and/or credit card</u>: A great way to get cash is with an ATM card, or you may want to have a CC with you. But be aware that many vendors do not accept them and prefer cash, especially for small purchases. In rural Italy it's best to have cash. Make sure you tell your bank or CC company that you will be traveling abroad so they don't block your card for suspicious activity.

TIPS FOR TRAVELING IN ITALY
(for first time visitors)

ACCOMMODATIONS (*ACCOGLIENZA*)

(Along the St. Francis Camino there are a number of simpler religious options for accommodations, as well as nicer hotels offering a variety of levels of comfort or simplicity. Therefore, the following tips are pertinent depending on the level of accommodations you choose.) Note that Italians are generally accustomed to smaller spaces than North Americans; therefore, rooms and bathrooms may be smaller with fewer amenities than what you are used to. Some do not offer hair dryers, so you may want to bring one (with appropriate adapter and converter). Essential toiletries, like shampoo, hand soap, and towels, are usually provided. Given European environmental regulations (plus the high cost of energy) usage of air conditioning and heating is limited by law. Some pilgrims use earplugs to help them sleep at night given the noisy character of Italian towns and guests. Tap water in hotels is always safe to drink in Italy. Wi-Fi nowadays is usually available in most hotels, and even simpler religious accommodations. For electric-powered items, such as hair dryers, you will need to bring both a transformer and adapter, as European household electricity operates at 220 volts (US is 110 volts). Often cell phone or digital camera battery chargers will operate off 220v or 110v and will not need the transformer, but still require the adapter to plug in.

MONEY (*SOLDI*)

Italian currency is in Euro (€). Once in Italy, an easy way to get Euros is through an ATM machine with an ATM bank card. Credit cards may be an option for payments, though merchants are sometimes reluctant to accept them, especially for smaller purchases. It is recommended to contact your financial institution to find out what charges will be incurred for using your

ATM or credit card in Italy; also let them know that you will be using your card in Italy, otherwise they might consider your overseas charges as suspicious and block the card. Traveler's checks are virtually obsolete nowadays as few banks redeem them anymore. Beware that currency exchange booths in Italy sell Euros at low rates and charge high fees.

MEALS (*PASTI*)

The Mediterranean diet was recently declared as having cultural value for the world by UNESCO. Nonetheless, schedules and quantities are different from what many English-speaking people are accustomed to. Breakfast (*prima colazione*) is served first thing in the morning and is continental; those used to a hearty breakfast will discover that Italian breakfasts are light and rich in pastries and cakes with some fruit, crackers, toast, jam, butter, cereal, or occasionally cold cuts and sliced cheese, always with copious amounts of espresso or cappuccino (bacon and eggs are only served in areas catering to international clientele or upscale hotels). Lunch (*pranzo*) is the main meal of the day for Italians, but most pilgrims usually forgo the heavy lunch for a similar meal at dinnertime at the hotel or in a local restaurant. Meals are served in courses. Appetizers are served first, such as bruschetta, soup or cold cut salamis or prosciutto with cheese. Next is the first course (*primo piatto*) which is usually pasta (or occasionally rice or polenta, more typical northern dishes). After the first course is the main course (*secondo piatto*) consisting of meat like pork, chicken, beef, or veal (fish, rabbit or horse is not uncommon for locals, but probably won't be served to foreign visitors). The main course is accompanied by a *contorno*, or side dish – often a vegetable or salad. Dessert (*dolce*) is regularly fruit, but can be ice cream, cake, or a pastry. Italians drink wine or water during meals, though soft drinks are sometimes available; North American visitors should note that ice is virtually never served in drinks in Italy. An espresso or liqueur may follow a meal. Italian society slows down considerably after lunch (for the siesta or *riposo*), and many businesses and most churches close from around 1:00 until early midafternoon, though nowadays in the big cities and touristy areas, shops and the important churches remain open. Italians eat late dinners, often around 8:00pm, and restaurants are often not open before 7:00. Most restaurants and hotels in Italy are accustomed to preparing food for participants with food allergies (like gluten-free or dairy-free), though some places in the more rural areas may not be equipped. For vegetarians, cheese is frequently the meat substitute.

PASSPORT (*PASSAPORTO*)

A current passport is required for international travel. To enter Italy, your passport should be valid for at least six months after your scheduled return date (in line with other Schengen countries). US, Canadian, and Australian citizens do not need a visa to enter Italy. If you are not a citizen of one of these countries, check with the Italian consulate to see if you will need a visa.

CHURCHES (*CHIESE*)

Despite abundant artwork, churches are places of worship and not museums. Some of the large basilicas utilize hired personnel to ensure visitors are dressed appropriately: dresses or shorts above the knees are not permitted, nor are sleeveless shirts. Taking photographs is permitted inside some churches but prohibited in others (including most churches in Assisi). Flashes should never be used on paintings, as they can damage artwork; however, they may be permitted on stone mosaic.

TIME ZONE/JET LAG (*FUSO ORARIO*)

The Italian time zone is Greenwich Mean Time plus one hour. From the US, it is six hours ahead of the Eastern Time zone, and they observe daylight savings time just as in the US. So, at 8:00 am in New York, it is 2:00 pm in Italy. Italians typically use a 24-hour clock instead of am/pm, thus 5:00 pm is written 17:00.

MAIL (*POSTA*)

Stamps may be purchased in Italy at tobacco shops (designated with a large 'T') or at the Post Office. Stamps to send letters to the US cost 1.20 cents (in euros).

PUBLIC RESTROOMS (*BAGNI PUBBLICI*)

Public restrooms are identified by WC (water closet). Note that public restrooms sometimes require a small fee to use. Sometimes public restrooms lack toilet tissue, so we recommend carrying tissue with you. Shop owners are generally reluctant to allow people to use their restroom without purchasing something.

SHOPPING (*LE SPESE*)

Shops are normally open from 9:00 am to 1:00 pm and then from 3:00 or 4:00 pm to 8:00 pm. However, in large and tourist areas they usually remain open continuously. Italian customer service is generally lousy. Also, note that store windows are for "browsing" and Italian merchants often expect you to purchase something if you enter. Italian cashiers are often short on change, and they prefer small bills or the exact amount. Sales tax is included in the advertised price. To discourage tax evasion, by law you must keep your receipt within 100 meters of the store, although this law is rarely enforced.

OBTAINING THE PILGRIM'S PASSPORT

The Pilgrim's Passport (*Credenziale* in Italian), will be a memorable, if not mandatory, keepsake for your Camino. There are spaces in which to receive stamps at each stage of the journey. At a minimum, you should have your accommodations place a stamp in it each night; many hotels catering to pilgrims have created their own stamp specifically designed for the Camino; otherwise, every business establishment in Italy will have an official business stamp that can be used. (Note that the proprietor is supposed to sign and date the stamp, but it is not mandatory.)

The *Credenziale* is necessary to receive your final *Testimonium* (Certificate of Completion) at the end of your journey, as it serves as the official record of the distances you have walked. Note that a minimum of one hundred kilometers are necessary to receive the *Testimonium*, and they do not have to be contiguous. It should be shown at your destination when you arrive (see below).

There are several ways to obtain the *Credenziale*, as there are at least two different Pilgrim Passports.

The official *Credenziale* as designed for the Camino of St. Francis by the Umbrian Episcopal Conference can be mailed to pilgrims in North America through an association in the US dedicated to serving pilgrims walking the Italian Caminos, including the St. Francis Camino: www.americanpilgrimstoitaly.org

For English-speaking pilgrims outside the US or Canada, you can request it directly from the official Italian pilgrim association responsible for distributing them:
www.piccolaccoglienzagubbio.it

Be forewarned that the Italian agency is not always prompt at responding to emails; additionally, there can be delays in international mail service. Therefore, you should order your Pilgrim's Passport well in advance (two to three months early is not unreasonable).

Otherwise, you can pick up a different *Credenziale* Passport directly at the Basilica of St. Francis just before beginning your Camino. The Pilgrim's Office, *Statio Peregrinorum*, just outside the main door to the lower basilica of St. Francis is there to serve pilgrims, keep track of official numbers of pilgrims walking, and distribute the *Credenziale* Passports. Note that the *Credenziale* issued at the Basilica is more generic than the other one and is designed for several different Caminos in central Italy. The *Statio Peregrinorum* closes during mid-day and closes continuously during the winter months from late November until early March. However, there is also an information office in the pilgrim's square before the lower basilica that remains open and can distribute Passports. Regardless of which *Credenziale* you use, either will suffice to receive your *Testimonium*.

Finally, a way to feel spiritually connected to the pilgrimage is by attending the Pilgrim's Mass at the Basilica of St. Francis. Each evening at 6:00 pm, the

Basilica salutes and offers prayers and a blessing to those departing on the Camino. Though in Italian, it is a special way to receive prayers and feel a part of the local pilgrim community. If you email your name to the basilica (at least one week in advance of your arrival), tell them which Mass you will be attending, and they will read your name at the end of the Mass and give you a special blessing.

Email: statioperegrinorum@sanfrancescoassisi.org

GPX TRACKS

A GPX Track is an electronically recorded route created with computerized GPS plotting. Anyone can create them with a GPS device which records timestamped GPS coordinates, plotted every 5 or 10 seconds, which are then connected to form a line. The tracks can be uploaded onto a device — like a cell phone app or handheld GPS device — which will then display the route as a line for you to follow.

The official St. Francis Camino GPX tracks have been recorded by the organizers of the Camino and are easily available for download.

GPX tracks are extremely useful — I would say even required equipment!!! Once uploaded onto a GPS unit or a smartphone, your route is depicted as a colored line on a map and your actual position as a dot. All you have to do is make sure the dot (which moves on the map as you move) stays on the colored line, and you will stay on the trail. This, in addition to the yellow/blue markings, signposts, and a good English guidebook will assure you won't get lost.

How to use GPX tracks

First, obtain the GPX tracks which are available online at: www.stfrancispillgrimages.com, or by contacting Bret Thoman at: bret@stfrancispilgrimages.com.

The most reliable way to follow GPX tracks is with a handheld outdoor GPS unit (like a Garmin or TomTom). Outdoor GPS units are fairly economical: a small Garmin (like etrex 10x/20x/30x) retails in the $120-$250 range. If you are planning on bringing or purchasing your own GPS device, you should upload the GPX tracks directly onto the GPS from your computer according to the instructions specific to the model. Just make sure the device comes with a map of Italy loaded onto the device, or else obtain one online or through the manufacturer's website. The advantages of using an actual GPS device is that they are specifically designed for GPS navigation (unlike cell phones that utilize Apps and can be sometimes glitchy), they have a long battery life, and they are small and convenient. The disadvantages are that unless you want to invest a lot of money, the screens are small and difficult to see on the trail. Also, handheld GPS units are designed for outdoor enthusiasts and have many more features than a casual one-time Camino walker needs. So, if all you want to do is read GPX tracks for this pilgrimage, a GPS unit may be a superfluous expense.

Therefore, a ridiculously economical (even free) option is to simply install a GPX file-reading App onto your smartphone. Today virtually all smart phones are equipped with GPS receivers which are activated when you turn on the location feature. Therefore, assuming you have a smart phone, you only need an appropriate App to read the GPX tracks.

<u>Android phones</u>

Let's start with Android-operated phones, such as Samsung. There are numerous GPX file-viewing Apps on the market, but an easy one to work with is **ViewRanger**. It is free and fairly simple to use. After you have downloaded the App through Play Store, open it. The first step is to load the map on your phone. Go to the options icon in the upper right screen, then click Maps. The best map is "ViewRanger Landscape". Open it. It will have you zoom in to narrow the section of the map you wish to load at a time. You may have to do this several times throughout your Camino walk.

Next, load the GPX tracks onto your phone. Open **ViewRanger** and go to the options icon in the upper right screen. Click "Import/Export"; then "Import externally". Now, find the folder/directory where the tracks are saved and click the file. It will load the track to your phone and will stay there until deleted. Next, click the map icon, scroll to Italy, and you will see the tracks on your phone.

Apple iPhones

Now let's move on to iPhones. The best GPX-reading App for iPhones is **MotionX**. It costs only $1.99, and is well worth it, as you get a lot for that price. It is fairly user friendly, you can store up to 300 tracks, easily record tracks and share them, and see stats for your activities.

1. Go to App Store and purchase the **MotionX** App.
2. Once you download it, make sure you answer yes to: "Always allow the App to access your location".
3. From within your iPhone, access your email inbox (or wherever the tracks are stored) and open the email(s) with the GPX files.
4. Click the GPX file(s) in your email app.
5. Locate and click the download icon.
6. Select the app you want to open the file with, which is **MotionX**.
7. Now click the green "Import" button at the top of the screen.
8. Go to Home page, click "Menu", and click on the specific track you wish to use.

Note that while the **MotionX** app does not save the map of Italy onto your phone, it does save a memory of the portion of the map you need when you open it initially with Wi-Fi. Thus, you will have the map overlay feature even if you do not have roaming data turned on while you are walking.

A word of caution: GPS apps drain cellphone batteries fast (particularly iPhones). Therefore, make sure your smart phone is fully charged before you set out each morning. And if you are planning on relying on your smart phone to navigate, I highly recommend bringing a portable battery charger with you, especially for long days on the trail. Finally, to save battery life, it is recommended to keep the phone turned off and only activate the App if you are in doubt as to your whereabouts.

A WORD OF CAUTION

Though the St. Francis Camino may seem romantic and inviting, a word of caution is in order: this is a physically demanding Camino. As much of the geography between Assisi and Rome is characterized by the Apennine Mountains, there is no way to make the trail easy. Daily distances range from 18 to 25 kilometers (8-16 miles). But apart from the distances, it's the elevation changes that make it all the more challenging. There are some sharp climbs and descents in excess of 600 meters (2,000 feet), in addition to some stretches on narrow switchbacks on loose shale that can be treacherous when wet. All this makes for some serious mountain hiking! But even when you are out of the mountain ranges, there is no shortage of hills on each day's stage.

Thus, the entire route from Assisi to Rome (roughly 14 days) should only be attempted by expert hikers who have significant mountain experience and are in excellent physical shape.

However, for those pilgrims not looking for an extreme mountain Camino, there are ways to make it less intense. Taxi service or public transportation can be utilized to avoid the most challenging stages. Also, there are luggage transport services that can be arranged to move your suitcase from hotel to hotel while you carry only a day pack.

If you want to avoid the most difficult stages, I recommend opting for the easier stage from Assisi to Spello, or else taking a taxi up to the Carceri hermitage. Another difficult day is the stage from Spoleto to Macenano (which involves a 600-meter climb up to the hermitage of Monteluco followed by a steep descent into the Nera Valley). Still another mountain climb (where there is little cell phone service) is from Piediluco to the town and hermitage of Poggio Bustone.

If you have only four or five days available and wish to focus on the most rewarding parts of the Camino, I would recommend walking through the Spoleto Valley from Assisi to Spoleto (four days, 60 km), or walking the four Franciscan hermitages in the Rieti Valley including Poggio Bustone, La Foresta, Fonte Colombo and Greccio — also four days.

Regardless of which route you choose, it is essential to prepare properly prior to departure. A good training regime ahead of time will help not just aerobically and with muscle tone for the hills, but it can also help prevent falls and injuries.

Additionally, if your feet are not accustomed to walking long distances potentially in the heat, blisters will be the result. The best way to prevent blisters is by training beforehand and breaking in hiking boots or shoes. This may be even more important than adequate aerobic training, since painful blisters can easily bring an end to a much-desired Camino.

Next, the time of year for your pilgrimage should be considered carefully. Weather in Italy varies considerably: summers are hot, winters cold, and the fall and spring seasons vary. Walking in the summer months of July and August is not recommended as there is the real risk of extreme heat; if you must go during the summer, many pilgrims begin walking early in the morning to beat the mid-day's heat seeking to arrive at destination no later than noon.

The winter months are not recommended either, as (apart from the cold temperatures and potential snow at altitude) light is an issue. When the clock changes to standard daylight time (at the end of October), dusk sets in around 4:30 pm. However, in the shadow of the mountains or on overcast or drizzly days, it can get uncomfortably dark as early as 3:30 pm. Thus, starting at daybreak will be crucial. Consider that on winter solstice, December 22, there are only a total of nine hours of daylight; you can calculate the amount of daylight on any given day roughly by adding two minutes per day both before and after December 22.

Next, pilgrims should be cautioned regarding wildlife. Wild boar are rampant in the mountainous and hilly stretches of the Apennines to the point of becoming a public nuisance (they're beginning to spread to the towns and even cities). Though in rare circumstances they can be aggressive (perhaps if they have piglets nearby or if they feel cornered or otherwise trapped), they virtually always flee when people are within earshot.

A more assured encounter, in any case, will be with dogs. A common sheepdog in central Italy is a large white dog known as an Abruzzese Shepherd or locally as a Maremmano. These dogs are used to protect and herd flocks of sheep usually in pairs and sometimes with the presence of a pastor. Other times, locals use them as guard dogs for their country houses. These dogs are bred to protect their sheep and properties and will do so if they sense a threat. Therefore, if you see a flock of sheep, though it may be tempting to get close to them for a selfie, it is best to move away when there are sheepdogs present.

Also, be alert when walking through areas of fenced properties; sometimes the fences have openings or other times the dogs are wandering about the streets in the vicinity of their houses. Thus, exercise caution if you come upon a pack of unleashed or unfenced dogs. Though dog bites are rare, pilgrims have been, unfortunately, bitten.

Lastly, the dreadful venomous viper, or European asp, should not be omitted. Now I have never actually seen such a snake, despite having traversed many kilometers throughout central Italy. Yet, a favorable habitat of theirs is the dry, sunny areas in low mountains and hills throughout Italy. Though not lethal, a bite would necessitate immediate medical attention.

For these reasons – in addition to a fall or other injury – it is strongly recommended not to undertake the Camino alone. Additionally, it should be said that women have sometimes reported being subject to catcalling or other unwanted attention. Therefore, walking with at least one other companion will mitigate all such risks on the Camino.

SPIRITUALITY

PILGRIMAGE, THE JOURNEY

Life is a journey, a pilgrimage. The word derives from the Latin word, *peregrinare*, meaning "to wander through fields of grain." Pilgrimage seems to be almost instinctive to humankind. Throughout the centuries, people of all faiths and traditions have set out on sacred journeys or quests. Pilgrimages are present in classical and mythological literature; in the ancient Greek epic poem, The Odyssey, Homer recounts the ten-year voyage of Odysseus's return home after the Trojan War. They are innate to virtually all religious traditions: Hajj, pilgrimage to Mecca, is the fifth pillar of the Islamic faith, and the journey is a once in a lifetime requirement for every able-bodied Muslim; Buddhists make pilgrimages to Lumbini, the birthplace of the Buddha, Bodh Gaya, the place of his Enlightenment, Sarnath, where he delivered his first teaching, and Kusinagar, India where he died; Hindus have made pilgrimages to places associated with legendary events from the lives of various gods.

The Bible is filled with stories of God beckoning a person or groups of people to move forward from one place to another. The first biblical "pilgrimage" is recounted in Genesis 12: 1-4. Abram was called by Yahweh to leave his pagan past and his father's home in order to migrate to the land of God's choice, where he would receive divine blessings:

> The Lord said to Abram: 'Go forth from the land of your kinsfolk and from your father's house to a land that I will show you. I will make of you a great nation, and I will bless you; I will make your name great, so that you will be a blessing. I will bless those who bless you and curse those who curse you. All the communities of the earth shall find blessing in you.' Abram went as the Lord

directed him, and Lot went with him. Abram was seventy-five years old when he left Haran." (Genesis 12: 1-4); Read also: Exodus 12:37-19:8

In these stories, Abraham and Moses follow the voice of God who leads them out of the place they were. God calls them to go forth on a journey, at the end of which he gives them covenants. Abram leaves pagan Haran for Canaan, and later receives a new name, Abraham; Moses leaves Egypt where the Israelites were enslaved by the Pharaoh for Mount Sinai where God gives him the law. In both cases, the journey involved a long period of struggle, uncertainty, doubt, desert (literal and metaphorical), and difficulty in which they felt lost. However, in both cases, they ultimately arrived at a better place. Certain ideas are introduced – that of hearing the call of God, leaving, wandering as a foreigner or stranger in exile, and ultimately arriving in a purified place and state.

In the New Testament, similar themes of departure, exile, and arrival continue; however, they are largely focused on Jesus, and later, his followers. Jesus's human life on earth can be viewed as sojourner and stranger. His mission was the ultimate pilgrimage – a divine pilgrimage. The divine and human "journey" of Christ is summarized in the Nicene Creed:

We believe in one Lord, Jesus Christ, the only Son of God, eternally begotten of the Father, God from God, Light from Light, true God from true God, begotten, not made, one in being with the Father. Through Him all things were made. For us men and our salvation He came down from heaven: by the power of the Holy Spirit, He was born of the Virgin Mary, and became man. For our sake He was crucified under Pontius Pilate; He suffered, died, and was buried. On the third day He rose again in fulfillment of the scriptures: He ascended into heaven and is seated at the right hand of the Father. He will come again in glory to judge the living and the dead, and his kingdom will have no end.

Like the narratives of the Old Testament prophets, we see similar themes: Jesus, whose "kingdom was not of this world,"[1] listened to the voice of his Father, obeyed, and left his "home" by becoming incarnate in the world. In his worldly life as "sojourner" he identified with the prophets who also passed through this world as aliens and experienced suffering and exile. As Abraham and Moses "wandered" through the desert, Jesus on earth "had nowhere to rest his head."[2] His mission was to journey through the "foreign" land of this fallen world in order to redeem it and its inhabitants. And, like the prophets, Jesus ultimately went to a better place after his Resurrection; unlike them, however, Heaven was the place whence he had originally left. Jesus's mission was to make humanity heirs of the eternal kingdom through his Incarnation, Passion, and Resurrection. Thus, his pilgrimage took him full circle from his Father in heaven through the "insecurity" of earth and back to heaven.

And this is the struggle for Jesus's followers whom Christ called to have faith in and imitate him. Christians, like Jesus and the prophets, are also called to become "strangers and aliens on earth" (Hebrews 11: 14). Peter urged his followers: "as aliens and sojourners to keep away from worldly desires that wage war against the soul."[3] And "conduct yourselves with reverence during the time of your sojourning."[4] Yet, the state of exile is not the Christian's ultimate goal – Heaven is. Thus, the Christian calling is to remain pure and undefiled by the corruption of the world in hope of a better world to come.

It took some time before Christians began to interpret the Christian life as pilgrimage. In the first few centuries after Christ's death, there was little collective desire to return to Palestine to revisit the sites of Jesus's life. The first Apostles, on the contrary, left Palestine in an effort to spread the Gospel in all corners of the world. It was only after the fourth century AD, largely as a result of the legalization of Christianity, that pilgrimages began in earnest. After legislating Christianity's freedom in the Edict of Milan in 313 AD, the first Christian Roman emperor, Constantine, built large basilicas in Rome

---

[1] John 18:36
[2] Luke 9:58
[3] 1 Peter 2:11
[4] 1 Peter 1:17

over the tombs of Peter and Paul, as well as other basilicas in honor of Jesus, Mary, and John. Meanwhile, his mother, Helena, erected churches and shrines in Palestine to memorialize events from the Gospels. These large edifices paved the way for Christians to come and offered them space in which to worship. Additionally, Helena brought relics from Jerusalem back to Europe, sparking interest in the holy places of Jesus's earthly life. Thus, Christians from around the world slowly began to journey to the tombs of the martyred apostles in order to honor them, connect with the events of their lives, and do penance.

The Spanish nun or noblewoman, Egeria, in the late fourth century spent several years in the Holy Land and kept a diary of her observations of places she visited as well as the particular rites in Masses. In a letter now called *Itinerarium Egeriae*, this is the earliest written account of a Christian pilgrimage.

However, it wasn't until the eleventh century that the practice of pilgrimage became widespread and entered into Christian devotional practice. And without ignoring the violence of many crusaders, the stories told by them after returning home did much to give people a knowledge and desire to go to the sacred places of Jesus's life. And while the Holy Land was the main destination of pilgrimage in the beginning, in later centuries, huge numbers of Christians from all classes set out to Rome to visit the tombs and Basilicas of Peter and Paul, Compostela in Spain to visit the tomb of St. James, Loreto to the Holy House of Mary, Monte Sant'Angelo to the grotto where St. Michael the archangel appeared, and elsewhere.

In the year 1300 AD, Pope Boniface instituted the first Jubilee year granting a plenary indulgence to pilgrims who made the journey to Rome. The desire to go was so strong that the pilgrim risked disease, violence, shipwrecks, and strife. Few returned home as dangers were great, and pilgrims often settled down in other lands. So before setting off, the medieval pilgrim prepared a last will and testament, gave away or sold his/her possessions, and celebrated the Church's sending-off liturgical rite similar to that of a funeral. After donning the recognizable pilgrim's tunic with in-sewn cross, the walking staff, and leather pouch to carry food and money, the pilgrim set off on the journey. A broad-brimmed hat was used with a long scarf wrapped around the body from the back to the waist. The symbol of the scallop shell was worn on the tunics of those headed to the tomb of St. James in Compostela, while the keys were worn by those going to Rome. The distinctive dress set the pilgrims apart and identified them as such for protection.

Much of the motivation for traveling on pilgrimage in medieval times was to receive the indulgence, as the pilgrimage was considered a very important form of penance and as a way of internal purification in hopes of lessening punishment for sins. The indulgence required sacrifice, prayer, penance, and the arduous journey itself. During this time, monks began using pilgrimage as a metaphor for the inner journey of the heart and soul; they linked the outer external pilgrimage to the inner contemplative spiritual journey.

Other reasons for going on pilgrimage were to connect with saints to whom the pilgrim felt devoted. In the same way that today we commemorate the birth-home of a famous person with a plaque or monument, shrines and sanctuaries were built to mark places where certain spiritual events occurred. Such places were often linked to events in the life of a saint: the saint's birthplace, the site of his/her martyrdom or natural death, the place where he/she received a particular grace or experienced a mystical event, and the church or shrine containing the saint's relics. Thus, a pilgrimage to such shrines were methods of "re-living" such events.

Ultimately, pilgrimage had a goal: to encounter the living God. Therefore, pilgrimage was fundamentally about going to particular "holy" or "sacred" places in order to receive special graces through the spirituality or sacredness of place. In this, we have a Christian – yet firmly Franciscan – basis of the sacramentality of the world. This is important for the pilgrim who goes forth in the world, which was created good by God the Father through the Word, sanctified by the Incarnation and redeemed through the crucifixion of the Son. However, there is a paradox in this. We have discussed the calling and the journey of the Christian as being a "pilgrim and stranger" in the world. However, perhaps the Christian life is not one of complete exile and separation from God and heaven while on earth, in hope of a "future" heavenly reward. Perhaps Christ's promise of salvation was not "out there," but one that begins right now in this world. "For behold, the kingdom of God is among you."[5] Despite Francis's admonitions to remain as "pilgrims and strangers" in this world, didn't he seem to be quite at home in it? Didn't he seem to be already living the kingdom of Heaven within? Certainly, his attitudes towards creation, culminating in his Canticles of the Creatures, suggests his belief in the goodness of the world.

In fact, this has been called "spirituality of place," which has its origins in the theology of creation and the Incarnation. Assisi and other pilgrimage destinations are special, because they reveal an incarnate God – a God who comes among us. People have been touched by God in these places. By going to the places where our predecessors have experienced God, we can connect with the events and receive graces, too. Thus, the sacred places help us to connect with the living God – the God who "took on flesh and dwelt among us."[6]

Pilgrimage was dear to the hearts of Sts. Francis and Clare. Francis's pilgrimage began when he dedicated himself to the Christian life in the penitential tradition after rejecting the military life. He became a true "sojourner and stranger" when he left the security of his father's home as a young man and embraced a way of life of instability and insecurity through poverty. There are many references to the necessity of remaining as *pilgrims and strangers* written by Francis or about him. He wrote in his Rule: "Let the brothers not make anything their own, neither house, nor place, nor anything at all. As *pilgrims and strangers* in this world, serving the Lord in poverty and humility, let [the brothers] go seeking alms with confidence…"[7] He wrote in his Testament, "Let the brothers be careful not to receive in any way churches or poor dwellings or anything else built for them unless they are according to the holy poverty we have promised in the Rule. As *pilgrims and strangers*, let them always be guests there."[8] Thomas of Celano said, "He did not want the brothers to live in any place unless it had a definite owner who held the

---

[5] Luke 17:21
[6] Cf. John 1:14
[7] The Later Rule, Chapter 6, v. 2
[8] Testament, 24

property rights. He always wanted the *laws of pilgrims* for his sons: to be sheltered under someone else's roof, to travel in peace, and to thirst for the homeland."[9] The Assisi Compilation said of Francis: "He disliked anything in tables or dishes that recalled the ways of the world. He wanted everything to sing of *exile and pilgrimage*."[10] The Anonymous of Perugia and the Three Companions said of the brothers, "They went through the world as *strangers and pilgrims*, taking nothing for the journey."[11] (Italics are mine in these quotes.) Francis used the expression "follow the footprints of Christ" five times in four writings.[12] He journeyed numerous times on pilgrimage to Rome in order to visit the tombs of Peter and Paul; he went to the Holy Land several times; Bernard and Giles made a pilgrimage to the shrine of St. James in Compostela. And at Francis's beckoning, Pope Honorius III granted the plenary indulgence to the Portiuncula, making it a place of pilgrimage for all times.

Clare, like Francis, also left the stability and security of her father's home in order to embrace poverty. There is no record of Clare ever having made any geographical pilgrimage; however, she did send Lady Bona on pilgrimage to the church of St. James in Compostela in Spain.[13] Her mother, Ortulana, made pilgrimages to Rome, Monte Sant'Angelo in Apulia, and "beyond the sea," presumably to the Holy Land[14] – no small feat for a woman in the Middle Ages. Clare also quoted Francis in her own Rule using his same words, "Let the sisters not appropriate anything to themselves, neither a house nor a place nor anything at all; instead, *as pilgrims and strangers* in this world who serve the Lord in poverty and humility, let them confidently send for alms."[15]

The pilgrimage was the perfect metaphor for how the spiritual life should

---

[9] Thomas of Celano, 2nd Life, Chapter XXIX

[10] The Assisi Compilation, [24]

[11] Anonymous of Perugia, Chapter 9, v. 40 and Legend of the Three Companions, chapter XIV, v. 59.

[12] Cf. Cirino, Fr. Andre. "The Assisi Experience of 'Spirituality of Place'". *The Cord*, 47:1 (January-February 1997) 4.

[13] Process of Canonization of St. Clare: 17th witness

[14] Process of Canonization of St. Clare: First Witness

[15] Rule of Life, Chapter 7

be lived for Francis and Clare. In the Middle Ages, people's identities were based on class status and town citizenship, which they inherited through their families. By leaving the city walls of Assisi in order to stay in the valley with the lepers and marginalized, both Francis and Clare surrendered their earthly status and embraced their primary identity as "heirs" of the heavenly Father. By embracing a life of penance, they received their spiritual inheritance in the Father, which was, essentially, an identity in him.

Francis alludes to this in the *"First Letter to the Faithful,"* by claiming that those who do penance are related to God as his children, brothers, spouses, mothers, etc.; while those who do not do penance belong to the devil, "whose children they are and whose works they perform." He is claiming that one's worldly identity, i.e. class status is irrelevant to God; what makes one a child of God, according to Francis, is whether or not they are "in penance."[16]

Similarly, Clare, in her *Letters* to Agnes, wrote of following in the footprints of Jesus Christ. Being a radical follower of Christ in poverty created for Clare a new identity and set her apart in the world. The Privilege of Poverty so vigorously sought after by her was more about surrendering status and class than about trying to live like the poor or be poor. The only way a woman could be completely reliant on a providential God and allow herself to be vulnerable, was to move out of the protection of the cities and forbid property and endowments and the securities they provided. Thus, Clare saw her life as equivalent to that of Francis: by allowing God to provide for her as she journeyed through life and encountered what lay before her, she sought to embrace poverty.

Thus, in surrendering identity, class, status, security, and stability, the pilgrim was the perfect metaphor for how the Christian life should be lived for Francis and Clare. The pilgrim donned special clothes similar to that of a penitent, traveled poorly, and depended on the alms of others.[17] By surrendering material things of the world and placing their trust and hope completely in God's providence, the pilgrim voluntarily embraced a state of

---

[16] By "penance" Francis means "conversion."
[17] Cf. Armstrong, Regis. "Francis of Assisi, The Founder, The Early Documents." Footnote A, p. 136

insecurity and instability. Like the pilgrims, Francis and Clare chose poverty, instability, and insecurity at the foundation of their spiritual life because it demanded faith in God's providence.

Long after the death of Francis and Clare, pilgrimage continued to persist and had a lasting impact on culture and society. The father of the Italian language, Dante (a Third Order lay Franciscan), wrote his masterpiece, *The Divine Comedy*, between 1308 and his death in 1321. It is the first major work of Italian literature written not in Latin, but in the vernacular dialect spoken in Tuscany. In the poem, Dante narrates his travels through Hell, Purgatory, and Heaven. At a deeper level, however, it is an allegorical journey of the soul towards God. It began with the following lines:

*Nel mezzo del cammin di nostra vita
mi ritrovai per una selva oscura
ché la diritta via era smarrita.*

At the midpoint of the journey of our life
I found myself in a dark forest
because the straight path was lost.

Dante begins his poem as a *pilgrim and stranger*. His journey is complete only when he arrives in Heaven; like the prophets of old, he is called to pass through a "desert" only to arrive at a better place.

Of course, not every pilgrimage was from the outset an intense spiritual undertaking, and some were more "profane" in nature. In the English language, Geoffrey Chaucer, writing in the same century as Dante, wrote "The Canterbury Tales." In this Middle English classic, he recounts the episodes of a group of pilgrims as they traveled from Southwark to the shrine of Saint Thomas Becket at the Cathedral of Canterbury, England. Each pilgrim takes turn telling stories in a contest. The book is a wonderful close-up look at real medieval pilgrims, some holy, some not, some looking for a good time, others for genuine holy experience. The prologue begins by saying that people desire to go on pilgrimage in the springtime when nature is coming back to life after the dead of winter. *(The following version is adapted into modern English.)*

> When April with his showers sweet with fruit
> The drought of March has pierced unto the root
> And bathed each vein with liquor that has power
> To generate therein and sire the flower;
> When Zephyr also has, with his sweet breath,
> Quickened again, in every holt and heath,
> The tender shoots and buds, and the young sun
> Into the Ram one half his course has run,
> And many little birds make melody
> That sleep through all the night with open eye
> (So Nature pricks them on to ramp and rage)-
> Then do folk long to go on pilgrimage,
> And palmers to go seeking out strange strands,
> To distant shrines well known in sundry lands.
> And specially from every shire's end.

Devotional geographical pilgrimages fell into decline after the Protestant Reformation which challenged the theology of the Indulgence, as well as medieval devotions. In the 17th century, John Bunyan, a Puritan jailed for preaching without a license in Anglican England, used pilgrimage as allegory in his tale, "The Pilgrim's Progress." In this enduring work (it was recently made into a movie), Bunyan offers insight in the Christian life by narrating the temptations and pitfalls of Christian, the Pilgrim, as he journeys to Celestial City and meets Evangelist, Charity, Hypocrisy, Goodwill, Obstinate, Mr. Worldly Wiseman, and more characters along the way.

The Enlightenment of the 18th and 19th centuries virtually eliminated the devotional pilgrimage as modern people rejected it as a medieval superstition lacking in reason. At about the same time, modern tourism was born in the form of the classical Grand Tour. Lasting several months, this tour was the foundational part of the education of European young men (mostly British) from well-to-do families. The itinerary exposed them to the classical antiquities of Rome and Greece as well as the Renaissance art cities of southern Europe. It was predominantly educational, not spiritual, in nature. The Grand Tour flourished until the advent of the railway, which afforded people of lesser economic status the possibility of traveling.

In the past few decades, interest in pilgrimage has increased, and modern pilgrims have once again sought out the spiritual dimensions of the faith journey. Money, leisure, and especially the jet airplane have opened the doors to travel to many people today who could have only dreamed of such a journey in generations past.

Certainly, the conditions and motivations of pilgrimages are quite different from those of Abraham and Moses, and Francis and Clare: jets, luxury coaches, and modern hotels have rendered the journey less perilous and penitential. Nonetheless, jet lag, sore feet, and the absence of the comforts of home can still demand patience. Despite the differences, however, the pilgrimage remains a response within the soul to move closer to God – to leave the ordinary in order to embrace the unknown within the context of faith. Modern pilgrims may be less concerned with earning indulgences, but they are still seeking that inner transformation that accompanies the journey. They still set out to the tombs of the apostles and martyrs, sites of apparitions and locutions, and the birthplaces of their favorite saints. Today's pilgrims often want to free themselves of restraints at home in order to find God without clutter in their lives; they hope to witness miracles, signs, and truth; they often wish to find an answer to their heartfelt prayers. A pilgrimage to a holy place is still a way to find answers to such prayers, though sometimes God's answer is different from the one we seek.

In summary, pilgrimages are a calling from God to the journey. Pilgrimage involves a process of departure, wandering, and arrival. It entails a sense of rupture when the pilgrim leaves what is familiar and enters a new place where they become, in the biblical words so often quoted by Francis and Clare, a *"pilgrim and stranger."* However, at some point on the journey, that feeling of being a stranger passes, and a sense of familiarity rekindles within. It may happen during the wandering, upon arrival, or even after returning home. And in the process, the pilgrim becomes something they were not before, as they arrive home transformed. They have gone through the same inner spiritual journey as the prophets and pilgrims of yesterday and are no longer the "old man"; the pilgrim is "renewed."[18] The pilgrim has moved through loneliness, exile, sin and wandering to grace, purpose, reassurance and wholeness in God.

The calling of a Christian is to set out and follow the footsteps of Christ as a pilgrim. And the Christ whom we follow became incarnate in a broken world to redeem its fallen, sinful nature. Yet, at the same time Christ penetrated it as the center point of all creation to reveal the might and wonder of God the Father. In the same way, your pilgrimage may at times be risky as you encounter unsuspected difficulties in an unfamiliar land that is sometimes scarred and broken – one that is "groaning and crying out."[19] Nevertheless, the same land will reveal a world created by God that is beautiful beyond imagination – "a place of wellsprings."[20] So whether you are preparing for an actual journey to Assisi or your journey will be "inward" and take place in your home, it is my hope and prayer that your life will be enriched and transformed as a result of it.

Thomas Merton, in his classic autobiographical work, *Seven Storey Mountain*, sums up pilgrimage in the following words.

In one sense we are always traveling, and traveling as if we did not know where we were going. In another sense we have already arrived. We cannot arrive at the perfect possession of God in this life, and that is why we are traveling and in darkness. But we already possess Him by grace, and therefore, in that sense, we have arrived and are dwelling in the light. But oh! How far have I to go to find You in Whom I have already arrived!

---

[18] Romans 6:6; Ephesians 2:15; 4:22-24; and Colossians 3:9-11
[19] Romans 8:18-25
[20] Psalm 184

Ask the Lord now to bless you as you embark on the journey. And, in the words of Mark Twain, "Twenty years from now you will be more disappointed by the things you didn't do than by the ones you did do. So throw off the bowlines. Sail away from the safe harbor. Catch the trade winds in your sails. Explore. Dream. Discover."

FROM FRANCIS TO PETER — FROM THE TAU TO THE KEYS

Assisi: City of St. Francis

Assisi is a beautifully preserved fortified medieval hill town famed throughout the world as the birthplace of St. Francis. It is visited annually by millions of pilgrims and tourists alike for its spiritual atmosphere and artwork.

Assisi is an ancient city of ancient Umbrian origins and owes its name to the Romans who called it Asisium. Its inhabitants converted to Christianity in the third century and it later fell under imperial control of the Lombard and Frankish Duchy of Spoleto. In the late twelfth century the citizens (mostly merchants or commoners) rebelled, establishing a "*comune*," a city-state or free municipality. Later in the middle ages, the city became known as Ascesi (from the root, ascend), and in modern times it was called as it is today, Assisi.

Francis was born during the winter of 1181-82 to Pietro di Bernardone, a successful cloth merchant admired for his astuteness in business and feared for his temper. His mother was a pious woman from Provence named Pica.

Assisi's most famous son lived a carefree youth replete with feasts, merriments and carousing with his companions – a lifestyle not uncommon to the young bourgeois men of his day. Admonished by his father for his largesse toward the poor and his disinterest in business affairs, Francis instead desired to become a knight.

His imagination was fired by the tales of minstrels who sang of the legends and heroic deeds of Galahad, Arthur, Lancelot, and Tristan. Dreaming of becoming like them, he sought to prove himself on the battlefield which would lead to knighthood and noble status. So, he joined the Assisi troops and rode on horseback with the knights in a battle against Perugia in 1199. Yet, it did not go as planned and instead of the glories of nobility and knighthood, Francis languished in a Perugian dungeon for a year.

After he was released, his thirst for worldly glory had not yet been extinguished and he went to war once again. He had a dream in which he saw himself in a glorious palace with arms and men he would lead in battle which, he believed, was a sign he was supposed to fight. So, he joined the forces of Sir Walter of Brienne fighting on behalf of the pope against the excommunicated German emperor, Otto. This time, however, Francis never made it to the battlefield.

After only one day's journey from Assisi, while in a dreamlike state overnighting in Spoleto, Francis heard a voice ask him if it was better to serve the Lord or the servant. Recognizing the voice of the true Lord, Francis understood obedience and listened. There, he renounced war, gave away his armor and weapons, and returned to Assisi to seek the will of God

Back at home, Francis became aware of an interior emptiness and he began to pray in caves around Assisi including the Carceri and the run-down church of San Damiano. There from the crucifix, he once again heard Christ speak to him and ask him to rebuild his house. He began to beg stones and mortar to rebuild dilapidated country churches around Assisi including San Damiano, St. Mary of the Angels, and St. Peter in Spina.

In a pivotal moment of his conversion, he embraced a leper. In the words of his biographer, "What before had seemed delightful and sweet had become unbearable and bitter; and what before made him shudder now offered him great sweetness and enormous delight." He left the security of his father's house and joyfully embraced poverty as a beggar and penitent.

Soon, others began following him: Bernard of Quintavalle, Peter Catani, and Giles. Together they served the poor and lepers in the plains below Assisi in an area known as Rivotorto. Later they set up huts around the small church of St. Mary of the Angels, also called the Porziuncola, which became the center of their new life and where friars have remained to this day.

In 1209 with his first twelve followers, Francis went to Rome to request ecclesial recognition for his way of life. Pope Innocent III orally approved the friars' way of life, recognizing the movement that would be called the Order of Friars Minor (Order of Lesser Brothers).

For the next twenty years Francis became a larger-than-life religious figure attracting more than five thousand men into his order. He traveled all over the known world preaching penance, negotiating peace, working miracles, serving lepers, and praying in hermitages.

Toward the end of his life, in 1224, at his beloved hermitage in Laverna, an extraordinary event took place. Brother Elias, the acting General Minister of the order, described the event in a public letter to the order upon Francis' death: "In the world, such a sign has never been heard, except in the Son of God, who is Christ God..." He was referring to the stigmata – the wounds of Christ – received by Christ on his body.

Two years later, on the night between October 3 and 4, 1226, Francis died peacefully on the bare ground behind his beloved Portiuncula. Just two years later he was canonized a saint and the next day Pope Gregory IX (formerly Cardinal Hugolino, the protector of the Franciscan Order) laid the foundation stone of the basilica to be built in his honor.

Francis' way of living the Gospel had an explosive impact on the culture of that time. By the end of Francis' life thousands of men had become friars, women's monasteries and convents everywhere were switching to the rule of Clare, and lay men and women everywhere were following Franciscan spirituality within their own homes, a so-called Third Order.

The story of Clare — lesser known than her male counterpart — began in the middle of the night on Palm Sunday 1212, when this eighteen-year old girl from a knightly Assisian family, left her home to become the first female follower of Francis. She went to the Porziuncola where Francis and the brothers met her and he tonsured her, shaved her head, marking her as a consecrated woman. From this encounter, a new movement — a second Franciscan Order — would emerge: that of penitential and evangelical women following the Franciscan way of life from within the enclosed cloister.

Today Assisi is celebrated throughout the world as the city of Francis and Clare and the cradle of Franciscan spirituality. As Rome is the political capital and Milan is the economic capital, Assisi is considered the spiritual heart of Italy. With St. Francis as the patron saint of the country, many Italians find in Assisi their spiritual heritage. When the earthquake of 1997 rocked the city, the country mourned the death of two friars and two laypersons who lost their lives in the basilica of St. Francis, in addition to the destruction of the basilica and city.

The spirituality of Assisi is not exclusive, and people of all nationalities and creeds have found a unique peace here. Even agnostics and skeptics leave Assisi feeling a little more spirited. And the city radiates such universal peace that it was only natural that the first inter-religious prayer meeting organized by Pope John Paul II (and continued by Pope Benedict) would be held here. In 2000, the Franciscan sites of Assisi were declared a world heritage site by the United Nation's UNESCO cultural department. Assisi is truly a blessed place for all.

The Tau represents Franciscan spirituality. Francis discovered the Tau symbol when he began serving lepers. Penitents in the Hospital religious order of St. Anthony, who had cared for lepers and other sick, also in the Assisi area, used the Greek letter drawn on their tunics as a sign of their penance.

Francis took to the meaning of this symbol so much that he adopted it as the symbol of his own penance (his conversion) and he saw himself as a "Champion of the Tau and of the Cross." He used the Tau as a kind of signature on letters he wrote, he painted it on places where he stayed, and drew it on his tunic. Today, despite its origins as a symbol of penance, it symbolizes Franciscan spirituality.

Rome: City of St. Peter

But who do you say that I am? Simon Peter said in reply, "You are the Messiah, the Son of the living God." Jesus said to him in reply, "Blessed are you, Simon son of Jonah. For flesh and blood has not revealed this to you, but my heavenly Father. And so I say to you, you are Peter, and upon this rock I will build my church, and the gates of the netherworld shall not prevail against it. I will give you the keys to the kingdom of heaven. Whatever you bind on earth shall be bound in heaven; and whatever you loose on earth shall be loosed in heaven."
(Matthew 16: 15-19)

Saint Peter was a fisherman with his brother, Andrew, from Bethsaida near the Sea of Galilee, and he was one of the first disciples to be called by Jesus. His life is featured prominently in the Gospels and the Acts of the Apostles, and he was with Jesus during significant events like the Transfiguration. He is always listed first among the twelve as he was assigned a leadership role by Jesus and acted as a spokesman among the Apostles. Early Christian writers provided more details about his life and asserted his primacy. Tradition describes him as the first bishop of Rome, the author of two canonical epistles, and a martyr under Nero, crucified head down and buried in Rome. His memoirs are traditionally cited as the source of the Gospel of Mark.

The book of Acts says that Peter left Jerusalem between 41 and 44 AD, during the persecution of Julius Agrippa, king of Judea and Galilee. Though Scripture doesn't say when he arrived in Rome to preach the Gospel in the capital city, it probably took place after 50 AD when the Christian community had already been established. Thanks to a letter written around 96 AD by St. Clement (the third successor of Peter), we know that Peter, like Paul, fell victim of the persecution of Emperor Nero. Nero sought to blame the Christians for a fire in July of 64 AD that destroyed a great part of the city. And it was during this first wave of persecutions that Peter was crucified in the Vatican circus, or racetrack, where capital punishments took place during the games.

After St. Peter's execution, tradition says that local Christian community buried his body in a nearby cemetery, referred to as a necropolis by the pagans. A shrine, known as a Tropaion, was built over the spot where he was believed to be buried. For decades, centuries even, the Christian community paid homage to St. Peter at this spot.

When Emperor Constantine legalized Christianity in 313 AD in the Edict of Milan, he ordered the construction of a basilica over the existing shrine. The Vatican hill needed to be leveled in order to prepare the foundation, and in the process the tomb of Peter was covered and buried deeper underground. At the same time, another basilica was built over the tomb of Saint Paul where he was believed to have been buried along the Via Ostiense. Constantine also built basilicas in Rome dedicated to St. Mary Major and St. John in Lateran.

During the late fifteenth century, the Constantinian basilica of St. Peter's had fallen into disrepair and was no longer large enough to accommodate the crowds that were coming. Therefore, it was leveled for construction of a new basilica, the current one. More recently, in the 1940s, archaeological work was done underneath the basilica, partly to demonstrate that the church was indeed built over the "rock of Peter" as tradition had held for almost two millennia that St. Peter was buried underneath the main altar.

Indeed, archaeologists discovered the red *Tropaion* over a tomb with graffiti written in Greek attesting to the presence of Peter, as well as bone fragments believed to be those of St. Peter himself. The underground necropolis and parts of the tomb of Peter can be visited today through the Scavi office of St. Peter's. Thus, the pilgrimage to Rome, to the tomb of St. Peter, is not just a journey rooted in faith, it is also grounded in archaeology.

In Scripture (Matthew 16:18-19), Christ presents the "Keys" to Peter representing the power of binding and loosing on heaven and on earth. In time, the keys came to symbolize not only St. Peter, but also his successors — the Popes – and their ministries, as well as the city of Rome. The key symbolizes, thus, the care and government of the Church. In the Middle Ages, pilgrims journeying to Rome wore a key on their tunic.

The Camino of St. Francis is a journey between the Tau and the Keys. Some might say that the journey between the two great Christian cities – between the TAU and the Keys – is one that connects the heart with the head. For just as the body cannot live without a heart and a head, neither can the Church survive without both. Thus, the Camino of St. Francis is one that connects spirit with structure, charism with institution, anima with animus.

As you begin this pilgrimage, let these two symbols — the Tau and the Key — guide you not only on your journey over the next two weeks, but for the rest of your own journey.

THE PILGRIM'S MOTTO:

1. I am willing to be flexible.
2. I'm neither in control nor in a hurry.
3. I journey in faith, hope, and peace.
4. I know God will provide for me.
5. My goal is the journey, not the destination.
6. I joyfully accept today's sacrifices, challenges, and blessings.

PRAYERS FOR THE JOURNEY

Following are some prayers that you can use at the beginning of your journey and throughout the pilgrimage.

Use the prayers that you feel called to and through which you feel the movement of the Holy Spirit. Prayer should not be forced, but gentle and inviting.

Memorize some of the prayers and chaplets and recite them while you walk. You can also take breaks during your walks and pray the longer ones.

Though formal prayer is important, try to be mindful of the prayerfulness of each moment even in mundane things: walking, resting, creation and nature, art and culture, encountering others, eating, sleeping, preparation for each day – all are moments of prayer for encountering God.

At the Beginning of the Pilgrimage
In the tradition of pilgrimages, rites and rituals have long been important. Upon arrival at your starting point, it is important to spend time in prayer. If traveling with a group, group prayers would be appropriate; if you are by yourself, pray privately.

If you begin in Assisi, consider attending the Pilgrim's Mass at 6:00 pm each day at the Basilica of St. Francis in Assisi, (in Italian); otherwise, any local Mass would suffice.

As you begin your pilgrimage, take some time to reflect on the following questions:

- How do you feel as you journey from your home or starting point to the destination? Are you excited, tired, uncertain, prayerful, indifferent, or anxious?

- What is important or special to you about the goal of your pilgrimage, the sanctuary?
- Why have you decided to make this journey?
- What are your intentions for this pilgrimage?
- Do you have any hopes motivating you to go on this journey?
- What kinds of sacrifices have you made to be on this pilgrimage?
- Are you seeking healing from an illness or disease, an addiction or something psychological? Are you hoping to mend a relationship? Have you experienced loss? Or are you going through a significant life change?
- Are there habits, disordered attachments, or other areas of your life that you are hoping to surrender during this pilgrimage?
- Who introduced you to Christ, the Church, and/or your Catholic faith? Was it your parents, or a relative? Was there someone else who inspired you in your faith life as an adult? Did you have a mentor, or guide? Think of these people as your spiritual companion on the journey. What do you imagine they would say to you at this moment on your pilgrimage journey?
- Do you have any Scripture passages you return to often? Why those passages? If not, think of some verse in the Bible that is important to you right now. Memorize the verse and repeat it throughout the pilgrimage.
- Is there a longing in your heart you wish to bring to God during this pilgrimage? Something that seems so far off or impossible that you may doubt that it could come to reality?

As you begin your pilgrimage, bring all these intentions, prayers, desires, and hopes to God. And trust that God will answer your prayers.

The following beginning prayers can be said at the beginning of your pilgrimage, as well as each day before setting out.

Traditional Pilgrimage Prayer

All-powerful God,
you always show mercy to those who love you,
and you are never far away for those who seek you.
Remain with us, your servants,
as we prepare for holy pilgrimage,
and guide our way in accord with your will.
Shelter us with your protection by day,
give us the light of your grace by night,
and, as our companion on the journey,
bring us to our destination in safety.
Through Christ our Lord. Amen.

Pilgrim's Prayer of St. James, Patron of Pilgrim Travelers

(St. James the Apostle is considered the patron saint of pilgrims because in the Middle Ages, his tomb and shrine in Compostela in northwestern Spain, was one of the most traveled pilgrim routes in Christendom.

It is not known if St. Francis ever visited Compostela, although some believe he went there in 1217 after returning to Spain due to illness while seeking to go to the Holy Land.)

"O God, who brought your servant Abraham out of the land of the Chaldeans,
protecting him in his wandering across the desert, we ask that you watch over us, your servants,
as we walk in the love of your name on the St. Francis Camino.

Be for us our companion on the walk,
Our guide at the crossroads,
Our breath in our weariness,
Our protection in danger,

Our home on the Camino,
Our shade in the heat,
Our light in the darkness,
Our consolation in our discouragements,
And our strength in our intentions.

So that with your guidance we may arrive safe and sound at the end of the road
and enriched with grace and virtue we return safely to our homes filled with joy.

St. James, pray for us.
St. Francis, pray for us.
Sts. Peter and Paul, pray for us.
Saint Mary, pray for us.
Amen."

Before Setting out Each Day:

Lorica Prayer

(*This is an ancient Irish prayer attributed to St. Patrick, ca. 377 AD*)

"I arise today
Through a mighty strength, the invocation of the Trinity,
Through a belief in the Threeness,
Through confession of the Oneness
Of the Creator of creation.

I arise today
Through the strength of Christ's birth and His baptism,
Through the strength of His crucifixion and His burial,
Through the strength of His resurrection and His ascension,
Through the strength of His descent for the judgment of doom.

I arise today
Through the strength of the love of cherubim,
In obedience of angels,
In service of archangels,
In the hope of resurrection to meet with reward,
In the prayers of patriarchs,
In preachings of the apostles,
In faiths of confessors,
In innocence of virgins,
In deeds of righteous men.

I arise today
Through the strength of heaven;
Light of the sun,
Splendor of fire,
Speed of lightning,
Swiftness of the wind,
Depth of the sea,
Stability of the earth,
Firmness of the rock.

I arise today
Through God's strength to pilot me;
God's might to uphold me,
God's wisdom to guide me,
God's eye to look before me,
God's ear to hear me,
God's word to speak for me,
God's hand to guard me,
God's way to lie before me,
God's shield to protect me,
God's hosts to save me
From snares of the devil,

From temptations of vices,
From everyone who desires me ill,
Afar and anear,
Alone or in a multitude.

I summon today all these powers between me and evil,
Against every cruel merciless power that opposes my body and soul,
Against incantations of false prophets,
Against black laws of pagandom,
Against false laws of heretics,
Against craft of idolatry,
Against spells of witches and smiths and wizards,
Against every knowledge that corrupts man's body and soul.
Christ shield me today
Against poison, against burning,
Against drowning, against wounding,
So that reward may come to me in abundance.

Christ with me, Christ before me, Christ behind me,
Christ in me, Christ beneath me, Christ above me,
Christ on my right, Christ on my left,
Christ when I lie down, Christ when I sit down,
Christ in the heart of every man who thinks of me,
Christ in the mouth of every man who speaks of me,
Christ in the eye that sees me,
Christ in the ear that hears me.

I arise today
Through a mighty strength, the invocation of the Trinity,
Through a belief in the Threeness,
Through a confession of the Oneness
Of the Creator of creation.
Amen."

Guard Me on My Journey

"Like unto the cup and the wine, and the holy supper,
which our dear Lord Jesus Christ gave unto his dear disciples
on each day, may the Lord Jesus guard me in daytime,
and at night, that:
No dog may bite me,
No wild beast attack me,
No serpent strike me,
No tree fall upon me,
No water rise against me,
No firearms injure me,
No weapons, no steel, nor iron cut me,
No fire burn me, No false sentence fall upon me,
No false tongue injure me,
No rogue enrage me, and that no fiends, no witchcraft
Or enchantment may harm me.
Amen."

Scripture Praising God through Creation

"You visit the earth and water it, make it abundantly fertile. God's stream is filled with water; you supply their grain. Thus do you prepare it: you drench its plowed furrows, and level its ridges. With showers you keep it soft, blessing its young sprouts. You adorn the year with your bounty; your paths drip with fruitful rain. The meadows of the wilderness also drip; the hills are robed with joy. The pastures are clothed with flocks, the valleys blanketed with grain; they cheer and sing for joy (Psalms 65:10-14).

"Bless the Lord, all you works of the Lord, praise and exalt him above all forever. Angels of the Lord, bless the Lord, praise and exalt him above all forever. You heavens, bless the Lord, praise and exalt him above all forever. All you waters above the heavens, bless the Lord, praise and exalt him above all forever" (see Daniel 3:57-90)

Prayers and Exhortations of St. Francis

These prayers can be said during quiet moments, or times of rest, while walking.

The Prayer St. Francis Recited upon Entering Churches:

(This is a traditional prayer inspired from the Holy Thursday liturgy. Francis recited it upon entering churches, according to his Testament (4-5). Many Franciscans, in the example of St. Francis, say this prayer each time they enter and exit a church.)

"We adore You, Lord Jesus Christ, in all Your churches throughout the world, and we bless You, for through Your holy cross You have redeemed the world."

Prayer Before the Crucifix

(This prayer is mentioned in some of the original 13th-century sources; they all indicate that Francis prayed it at the foot of the wooden Byzantine crucifix within the abandoned church of San Damiano. Most likely he began saying it during the years of his early conversion, in 1205-1206, when he frequently visited the abandoned church of San Damiano. Many Franciscans today pray it before crucifixes within churches.)

"Most High, glorious God,
enlighten the darkness of my heart
and give me true faith, certain hope, and perfect charity,
sense and knowledge, Lord,
that I may carry out Your holy and true command. Amen."

Praises of God

(*After receiving the stigmata on Mt. Laverna in September, 1224, Francis wrote the following words on a parchment and gave them to his companion, Brother Leo, together with a blessing. The original parchment is conserved in the reliquary chapel within the Basilica of St. Francis. This is a good prayer to say while taking a break during the day's walks.*)

"You are holy Lord God Who does wonderful things.
You are strong. You are great. You are the most high.
You are the almighty king. You holy Father,
King of heaven and earth.
You are three and one, the Lord God of gods;
You are the good, all good, the highest good,
Lord God living and true.
You are love, charity; You are wisdom, You are humility,
You are patience, You are beauty, You are meekness,
You are security, You are rest,
You are gladness and joy, You are our hope, You are justice,
You are moderation, You are all our riches to sufficiency.
You are beauty, You are meekness,
You are the protector, You are our custodian and defender,
You are strength, You are refreshment. You are our hope,
You are our faith, You are our charity,
You are all our sweetness, You are our eternal life:
Great and wonderful Lord, Almighty God, Merciful Savior."

Blessing of Saint Francis to Brother Leo
(This is the blessing of St. Francis to Br. Leo.)

"May the Lord bless you.
May the Lord keep you.
May He show His face to you and have mercy. May He turn to you His
countenance and give you peace.
The Lord bless you.
Amen."

The Canticle of the Creatures
*(Francis wrote this Canticle toward the end of his life between 1224-25, while
he lay sick at San Damiano and was cared for by Clare and the Poor Sisters.)*

"Most high, all powerful, all good Lord!
All praise is Yours, all glory, all honor, and all blessing.

To You, alone, Most High, do they belong.
No mortal lips are worthy to pronounce Your name.

Be praised, my Lord, through all Your creatures,
especially through my lord Brother Sun,
who brings the day; and You give light through him.
And he is beautiful and radiant in all his splendor!
Of You, Most High, he bears the likeness.

Be praised, my Lord, through Sister Moon and the stars;
in the heavens You have made them bright, precious and beautiful.

Be praised, my Lord, through Brothers Wind and Air,
and clouds and storms, and all the weather,
through which You give Your creatures sustenance.

Be praised, my Lord, through Sister Water;
she is very useful, and humble, and precious, and pure.

Be praised, my Lord, through Brother Fire,
through whom You brighten the night.
He is beautiful and cheerful, and powerful and strong.

Be praised, my Lord, through our sister Mother Earth,
who feeds us and rules us,
and produces various fruits with colored flowers and herbs.

Be praised, my Lord, through those who forgive for love of You;
through those who endure sickness and trial.

Happy those who endure in peace,
for by You, Most High, they will be crowned.

Be praised, my Lord, through our sister Bodily Death,
from whose embrace no living person can escape.
Woe to those who die in mortal sin!
Happy those she finds doing Your most holy will.
The second death can do no harm to them.

Praise and bless my Lord, and give thanks,
and serve Him with great humility."

A Salutation of the Blessed Virgin Mary

(Thomas of Celano, Francis' first biographer, wrote that Francis "embraced the Mother of Jesus with inexpressible love, since she made the Lord of Majesty a brother to us. He honored her with his own Praises, poured out prayers to her, and offered her his love in a way that no human tongue can express" (Second Life, 198). This praise in honor of the Virgin is a witness of the great affection that Francis nurtured for the Mother of God.)

"Hail, O Lady,
Holy Queen,
Mary, holy Mother of God,
Who are the Virgin made Church,
chosen by the most Holy Father in heaven
whom he consecrated with His most holy beloved Son
and with the Holy Spirit the Paraclete,
in whom there was and is
all fullness of grace and every good.

Hail His Palace!
Hail His Tabernacle!
Hail His Dwelling!
Hail His Robe!
Hail His Servant!
Hail His Mother!

And hail all You holy virtues
which are poured into the hearts of the faithful
through the grace and enlightenment of the Holy Spirit,
that from being unbelievers,
You may make them faithful to God."

Prayer of Saint Francis

(The following prayer, typically attributed to St. Francis, was written most likely by a French Franciscan friar in the early 1900s and was popularized during World War I and II. Though not written by Francis himself, it is a lovely expression of the great saint's spirituality and desire for peace.)

"Lord make me an instrument of your peace.
Where there is hatred let me sow love.
Where there is injury, pardon,
Where there is doubt, faith,
Where there is despair, hope,
Where there is darkness, light,
And where there is sadness, joy.

O divine master grant that I may
not so much seek to be consoled as to console,
to be understood as to understand,
To be loved as to love.

For it is in giving that we receive
it is in pardoning that we are pardoned
And it's in dying that we are born to eternal life.

Amen."

Exhortation of Saint Clare

(Clare wrote this in her Second Letter to Blessed Agnes of Prague, whom she exhorted into an ever-deeper relationship with God.)

"What you hold, may you always hold.
What you do, may you do and never abandon.
But with swift pace, light step,

unswerving feet,

so that even your steps stir no dust,

go forward

securely, joyfully, and swiftly,

on the path of prudent happiness,

believing nothing

agreeing with nothing

which would dissuade you from this resolution

or which would place a stumbling block for you on the way,

so that you may offer your vows to the Most High

in the pursuit of that perfection

to which the Spirit of the Lord has called you."

Saint Francis' Meditation Prayer

(Francis frequently prayed this simple, short phrase,
almost like a mantra, over and over, in Latin:

"Deus meus et omnia" ("My God and my All!")

Saint Francis' Petition for Holiness

(The following comes from Francis' Earlier Rule of 1221,
sometimes referred to as the Regula non bullata)

"Therefore, let us desire nothing else, let us wish for nothing else, let nothing else please us and cause us delight, except our Creator and Redeemer and Savior, the one true God, Who is the Fullness of Good, all good, every good, the true and supreme good, Who alone is Good, merciful, and gentle, delectable and sweet, Who alone is holy and just and true, holy and right, Who alone is kind, innocent, pure, from Whom and through Whom and in Whom is all pardon, all grace, all glory of all the penitent and the just, of all the blessed who rejoice together in heaven.

Therefore, let nothing hinder us, nothing separate us, or nothing come between us.

Let all of us, wherever we are, in every place, at every hour, at every time of day, everyday and continually, believe truly and humbly and keep in our heart and love, honor, adore, serve, praise, and bless, glorify and exalt, magnify and give thanks to the most high and supreme eternal God, Trinity and Unity, the Father and the Son and the Holy Spirit, Creator of all, Savior of all who believe in Him and hope in Him and love Him, Who is without beginning and without end, unchangeable, invisible, indescribable, ineffable, incomprehensible, unfathomable, blessed, worthy of praise, glorious, exalted on high, sublime, most high, gentle, lovable, delectable, and totally desirable above all else forever. Amen."

Prayer for Enlightenment

(*This prayer is mentioned in several manuscripts. Francis prayed it at the foot of the crucifix of San Damiano after Christ spoke to him through it telling him to rebuild His house.*)

"Most High glorious God, enlighten the darkness of my heart and give me, Lord, a correct faith, a certain hope, a perfect charity, sense and knowledge, so that I may carry out your holy and true command. Amen."

The Franciscan Crown Rosary

(Recitation of the rosary as it exists today began around the thirteenth century, though monks and nuns of the commoner class had been reciting Paters and Aves already for many centuries. The traditional rosary most Catholics are familiar with comes from the Dominican tradition, though the Franciscans developed a similar rosary, known as the Franciscan Crown Rosary, in the 15th century or possibly earlier, with seven decades and mysteries.)

The Franciscan Crown Rosary begins simply by stating the first Joy and then praying one *Our Father* and ten *Hail Marys* while meditating upon it. This same is done for the other six joys. It is customary to conclude by adding two *Hail Marys* in honor of the 72 years that Our Lady is said to have lived on earth, and one *Our Father* and *Hail Mary* for the intentions of the Pope.

Mysteries: the Seven Joys of the Virgin
1) The Annunciation
2) The Visitation
3) The Nativity of Our Lord Jesus Christ
4) The Adoration of the Magi
5) The Finding of the Child Jesus in the Temple
6) The Appearance of Christ to Mary after the Resurrection
7) The Assumption and Coronation of Mary as Queen of Heaven

Daily Prayer to Guardian Angel

Many people are not familiar with St. Francis' devotion to angels. Yet, Thomas of Celano wrote: [Francis] venerated the angels with the greatest affection, for they are with us in battle, and walk with us in the midst of the shadow of death. He said that such companions should be revered everywhere, and invoked as protectors. [Francis] taught that their gaze should not be offended, and no one should presume to do in their sight what he would not do in the sight of others. And since in choir one sings the psalms in the presence of the angels, he wanted all who were able to gather in the oratory and sing psalms wisely. [Francis] often said that Blessed Michael should be especially honored because his duty is presenting souls to God. In honor of St. Michael, he would fast with great devotion for forty days between the Feast of the Assumption and St. Michael's feast day. For he used to say: 'Each person should offer God some special praise or gift in honor of such a great prince.'" (Thomas of Celano Second Life, 149)

"Angel of God My guardian dear To Whom His love Commits me here Ever this day Be at my side To light and guard To rule and guide. Amen."

Prayer to St. Michael the Archangel
(Though this prayer was composed by Pope Leo XIII in 1886, St. Francis had a deep devotion to St. Michael: he used to frequently pray and fast for forty-day "Lents" preceding the feast of St. Michael; in fact, he received the stigmata in Laverna at the end of such a fast; he once visited the grotto of St. Michael in Puglia but did not cross the threshold and enter as he did not feel worthy. This prayer to St. Michael is typically said daily.)

"Saint Michael Archangel,
defend us in battle,
be our protection against the wickedness and snares of the devil;
may God rebuke him, we humbly pray;
and do thou, O Prince of the heavenly host,
by the power of God, cast into hell
Satan and all the evil spirits
who prowl through the world seeking the ruin of souls.
Amen."

Reflections During the Journey:
During your pilgrimage journey, take some time to meditate on and consider the following questions. Use them to pray with and reflect upon.

These reflections can be made outside, in creation along the route, or inside a sanctuary or church.

- As you begin experiencing various pilgrimage sites, what things do you initially notice?
- Is your heart drawn to a particular area, icon, or statue?
- Be still in silence and consider four of the five senses as you enter the space. Allow your senses to guide your experience:
  - What sights do you see?
  - What sounds do you hear?
  - What do you smell?
  - How does the space feel to the touch?
- Allow the Lord to enter the silence in your heart. What spiritual experience in your past does this space remind you of?
- What imagery do you notice in this space?
- What Scripture passages are you reminded of in this space?
- What traditions, sacramentals, or prayers are you reminded of in this space?
- How will you remember this space? Is there a particular image, prayer, message, or person that you will use to commemorate this experience?

THE ST. FRANCIS
CAMINO ROUTE

THE DAILY STAGES

Note that the following route notes do not include step-by-step instructions for navigating; it is assumed the pilgrim is navigating with GPX, or a detailed guidebook.

Go online and enter the Relive Video link to watch a 30-second video of each daily stage.

Stage 1: From Assisi to Foligno (easier route)
Distance: 20 kilometers
Cumulative increase in altitude: + 301 m
Cumulative loss of altitude: - 429 m
Surface: asphalt road, gravel road, dirt trail
Time: 5 hours
Difficulty: Moderate
Relive Video: relive.cc/view/vr63ZxgVAdO

Stage 1a: Assisi to Foligno (harder route)
Distance: 22 kilometers
Cumulative increase in altitude: + 925 m
Cumulative loss of altitude: - 1034 m
Surface: asphalt, gravel, dirt trails
Time: 8 hours
Difficulty: Very Difficult
Relive Video: relive.cc/view/v36ArpRzYZq

Stage 2: From Foligno to Trevi
Distance: 13 kilometers
Cumulative increase in altitude: + 425 m
Cumulative loss of altitude: - 240 m
Surface: asphalt road, gravel roads
Time: 6 hours
Difficulty: Moderate
Relive Video: relive.cc/view/vYvE9PnNZwv

Stage 3: From Trevi to Poreta
Distance: 12 kilometers
Cumulative increase in altitude: + 410 m
Cumulative loss of altitude: - 430 m
Surface: asphalt road, gravel roads
Time: 5 hours
Difficulty: Difficult
Relive Video: relive.cc/view/vr63ZxgV48O

Stage 4: From Poreta to Spoleto
Distance: 15 kilometers
Cumulative increase in altitude: + 520 m
Cumulative loss of altitude: - 500 m
Surface: asphalt road, gravel roads
Time: 5 hours
Difficulty: Difficult
Relive Video: relive.cc/view/vLqeNV2MAdv

Stage 5: From Spoleto to Ceselli
Distance: 17 kilometers
Cumulative increase in altitude: + 641 m
Cumulative loss of altitude: - 663 m
Surface: dirt trails, gravel roads, asphalt roads
Time: 7 hours

Difficulty: Experts Only
Relive Video: relive.cc/view/vYvE9P5LGwv

Stage 6: From Ceselli to Arrone
Distance: 16 kilometers
Cumulative increase in altitude: + 221 m
Cumulative loss of altitude: - 248 m
Surface: asphalt roads, gravel roads, dirt trails
Time: 5 hours
Difficulty: Easy
Relive Video: relive.cc/view/vDqgJVxnBG6

Stage 7: From Arrone to Piediluco
Distance: 14 kilometers
Cumulative increase in altitude: + 294 m
Cumulative loss of altitude: - 152 m
Surface: asphalt roads, gravel roads, dirt trails
Time: 4.5 hours
Difficulty: Moderate
Relive Video: relive.cc/view/vZqNN5EZ93q

Stage 8: From Piediluco to Poggio Bustone
Distance: 22 kilometers
Cumulative increase in altitude: + 978 m
Cumulative loss of altitude: - 662 m
Surface: asphalt roads, dirt roads, dirt trails
Time: 8 hours
Difficulty: Experts Only
Relive Video: relive.cc/view/vevW7Z2EzGv

Stage 9: From Poggio Bustone to Rieti
Distance: 18 kilometers
Cumulative increase in altitude: + 395 m

Cumulative loss of altitude: - 745 m
Surface: asphalt road, gravel roads, dirt paths
Time: 7 hours
Difficulty: Moderate
Relive Video: relive.cc/view/vYvrDm1K7L6

Stage 9a: From Rieti to Greccio (*optional excursion*)
Distance: 24 kilometers
Cumulative increase in altitude: + 470 m
Cumulative loss of altitude: - 390 m
Surface: asphalt roads, gravel roads, dirt trails, country roads
Time: 7.5 hours
Difficulty: Difficult
Relive Video: relive.cc/view/vZqNN5oVE3q

Stage 10: From Rieti to Poggio San Lorenzo
Distance: 22 kilometers
Cumulative increase in altitude: + 499 m
Cumulative loss of altitude: - 377 m
Surface: asphalt roads, gravel roads, dirt trails, country roads
Time: 7 hours
Difficulty: Moderate
Relive Video: relive.cc/view/vXOnEyk1dBv

Stage 11: From Poggio San Lorenzo to Ponticelli
Distance: 23 kilometers
Cumulative increase in altitude: + 821 m
Cumulative loss of altitude: - 1015 m
Surface: asphalt road, gravel roads
Time: 8 hours
Difficulty: Very Difficult
Relive Video: relive.cc/view/vPv4JPdXm36

Stage 12: From Ponticelli to Monterotondo
Distance: 30 kilometers
Cumulative increase in altitude: + 690 m
Cumulative loss of altitude: - 871 m
Surface: paths, asphalt road, dirt roads
Time: 9 hours
Difficulty: Very Difficult
Relive Video: relive.cc/view/vWqBe2ZM9Y6

Stage 13: From Monterotondo to Monte Sacro
Distance: 19 kilometers
Cumulative increase in altitude: + 311 m
Cumulative loss of altitude: - 422 m
Surface: asphalt road, gravel roads
Time: 6 hours
Difficulty: Moderate
Relive Video: relive.cc/view/vRO7d49rnK6

Stage 14: From Monte Sacro to St. Peter's
Distance: 16 kilometers
Cumulative increase in altitude: + 158 m
Cumulative loss of altitude: - 168 m
Surface: urban sidewalks, bike paths
Time: 5 hours
Difficulty: Easy
Relive Video: relive.cc/view/vRO7d49kry6

PHOTOS

Stage 1: From Assisi to Foligno: a group prepares to set out from Assisi

Stage 1: From Assisi to Foligno: the Upper Basilica of St. Francis

Stage 1: From Assisi to Foligno: the Church of St. Mary over Minerva in Piazza del Comune

Stage 1: From Assisi to Foligno: the Tomb of St. Francis

Stage 1: From Assisi to Foligno (easier route): the entrance to Panzo

Stage 1a: Assisi to Foligno (harder route): the monastery of San Benedetto

Stage 1a: Assisi to Foligno (harder route): a view of the Sibylline Mountains from the summit of Mount Subasio

Stage 1a: Assisi to Foligno (harder route): the Spello aqueduct

Stage 1a: Assisi to Foligno (harder route): the historic center of Spello

Stage 3: From Trevi to Poreta: the ruined castle of Poreta

Stage 4: From Poreta to Spoleto: the letter written by St. Francis to Brother Leo

Stage 4: From Poreta to Spoleto: the Basilica of San Salvatore

Stage 5: From Spoleto to Ceselli: the cathedral of Spoleto

Stage 5: From Spoleto to Ceselli: the entrance to the convent of Monteluco

Stage 5: From Spoleto to Ceselli: the ancient Roman tablet
in the forest of Monteluco

Stage 7: From Arrone to Piediluco: the Marmore waterfalls

Stage 8: From Piediluco to Poggio Bustone: the village of Labro

Stage 8: From Piediluco to Poggio Bustone: in the summer months, herders move their cows into the higher elevations of the mountains, known as the *trasumanza*

Stage 8: From Piediluco to Poggio Bustone: the Franciscan convent of San Giacomo

Stage 9: From Poggio Bustone to Rieti: the town of Cantalice

Stage 9: From Poggio Bustone to Rieti: a local transports his wares with a pack animal

Stage 9: From Poggio Bustone to Rieti: shepherds move their
flocks in the environs of Rieti

Stage 9: From Poggio Bustone to Rieti: a local pasta dish in Rieti, known as *maltagliata*

Stage 9: From Poggio Bustone to Rieti: the geographical center of Italy (Piazza Centro d'Italia)

Stage 9: From Poggio Bustone to Rieti: the ancient Roman bridge over the Velino River

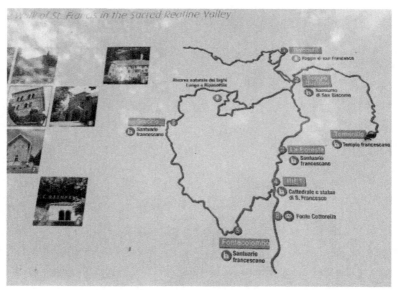

Stage 9a: From Rieti to Fonte Colombo and Greccio (*optional excursion*): a map showing the Rieti Valley walking trails connecting the four Franciscan convents

Stage 9a: From Rieti to Fonte Colombo and Greccio (*optional excursion*): ruined churches and hermitages dot the landscape along the way

Stage 9a: From Rieti to Fonte Colombo and Greccio (*optional excursion*): the convent of Fonte Colombo

Stage 10: From Rieti to Poggio San Lorenzo: a directional sign on the Roman Bridge over the Velino River in Rieti

Stage 10: From Rieti to Poggio San Lorenzo: an ancient Roman mile
marker from the era of Caesar Augustus

Stage 14: From Monte Sacro to St. Peter's: the welcoming Villa Borghese gardens adjacent to Piazza del Popolo

Stage 14: From Monte Sacro to St. Peter's: crossing Holy Angels Bridge

Stage 14: From Monte Sacro to St. Peter's: a Vatican official in the sacristy at St. Peter's prepares the well-deserved Testimonium

Stage 14: From Monte Sacro to St. Peter's: two pilgrims arrive in St. Peter's and collect their Testimonium

THE ROUTE

Stage 1: From Assisi to Foligno (easier route)
Distance: 20 kilometers
Cumulative increase in altitude: + 301 m
Cumulative loss of altitude: - 429 m
Surface: asphalt road, gravel road, dirt trail
Time: 5 hours
Difficulty: Moderate
Relive Video: relive.cc/view/vr63ZxgVAdO

When those that carried [Francis] came to the hospital [of San Salvatore], which is halfway on the road from Assisi to St. Mary's, he told them to [...] turn the litter towards the city of Assisi. And raising himself up, he blessed the said city.
(*Mirror of Perfection*, 124)

Daily Franciscan Spirituality/reflection: Pilgrimage

- *(If you walk the harder route to Foligno, use this reflection today, as well.)*
- Pilgrimage was dear to the heart of St. Francis. His pilgrimage began when he rejected the military life; he became a true "sojourner and stranger" when he left the security of his father's home and embraced instability and insecurity in poverty.
- Francis wrote about living as "pilgrims and strangers" frequently: "Let the brothers not make anything their own, neither house, nor place, nor anything at all. *As pilgrims and strangers* in this world, serving the Lord in poverty and humility, let [the brothers] go seeking alms with confidence…" (Rule of 1223, Chapter 6, 2); "Let the brothers be careful not to receive in any way churches or poor dwellings or anything else built for them unless they are according to the holy poverty we have promised in the Rule. As *pilgrims and strangers*, let them always be guests there" (Testament 24). Thomas of Celano wrote, "[Francis] did not want the brothers to live in any place unless it had a definite owner who held the property rights. He always wanted the laws of pilgrims for his sons: to be sheltered under someone else's roof, to travel in peace, and to thirst for the homeland." (*Second Life*, chapter 29) The Assisi Compilation said of Francis: "He disliked anything in tables or dishes, that recalled the ways of the world. He wanted everything to sing of exile and pilgrimage" (24). Legend of the Three Companions said of the brothers, "They went through the world as *strangers and pilgrims*, taking nothing for the journey" (chapter 14, 59). Francis used the expression "follow the footprints of Christ" five times in four writings. He journeyed numerous times on pilgrimage to Rome in order to visit the tombs of Peter and Paul; he went to the Holy Land several times; Bernard and Giles made a pilgrimage to the shrine of St. James in Compostela. And at Francis's beckoning, Pope Honorius III granted the plenary indulgence to the Portiuncula, making it a place of pilgrimage for all times.

- As you begin your Camino, reflect on how life mirrors pilgrimage. Look for similarities and consider how you can integrate the pilgrimage experience into your daily life.

Route notes:

- The easier route between Assisi and Spello is a gentle walk among olive groves on the "Sentiero degli Ulivi" (Olive Tree Trail) along the base of Mount Subasio.
- This route is not part of the official "Via di Francesco"; instead, it is part of a route called the CFM (Cammino Francescano della Marca), a Franciscan route from Assisi to Ascoli Piceno in the bordering region of the Marches. It is denoted by white and red stripes with acronym, CFM.
- Note also that some Guidebooks finish the first stage in Spello, while others continue to Foligno for overnight. You may wish to overnight in Spello, which would make the day's stage a little shorter.

The Route:

From Assisi's central square (Piazza del Comune), head towards the Basilica of Saint Clare. Continue straight and leave Assisi through the city gate known as Porta Nuova. Veer to the right and pass by the fuel station continuing straight through the next roundabout. At a Marian shrine, turn left and walk uphill past an elementary school and then through the newer residential area of Assisi.

Not long after passing Assisi's soccer stadium, on Via San Benedetto, you will note a dirt road to your left with signs indicating "Sant'Angelo in Panzo" as well as the street name, "Via Sant'Angelo in Panzo." Panzo is a hidden gem, its history unknown by most people even in Assisi. Clare came here for a short period of time after leaving San Paolo and before leaving for San Damiano.

Her sister, Agnes, joined her and Clare's first miracle took place here. The legends say that after Agnes arrived, her uncles and cousins arrived and sought to drag her away violently. But Clare went into the church and prayed. Then her sister's body became so heavy none of them, all knights, could lift her. After this ordeal, Francis accompanied the two sisters from Panzo to San Damiano where Clare remained until her death. Agnes was later sent to a community in Monticelli, near Florence, to lead as Abbess where she remained most of her life.

It may be worth walking an extra 250 meters each way to the end of this driveway for the chance to see the remains of the church now within the property of a noble Assisian family. Ring the bell and hopefully Rita, the caretaker, or her son will be there to open the gate and reveal the ancient church and beautifully manicured gardens, today utilized for receptions and other gatherings.

From the entrance way to Panzo, continue on the Camino away from Assisi. When you reach Via degli Ulivi, just north of the small village of San Vitale, you will pass two devotional shrines on your left. A lovely trail with views of the Valley of Assisi begins here, and the route alternates between paved roads and dirt roads. All around you are plenty of olive trees (the olive oil produced between Spello and Spoleto boasts a special DOP demarcation), and this road is known locally as the "Sentiero degli Ulivi" (The Olive Tree Pathway).

Here it is easy to see why the German writer and poet, Goethe, once wrote in 1786, while traveling through the Spoleto Valley, "The road to Foligno [from Assisi] along the side of the mountain overlooking the valley is beautiful, and my walk, which took fully four hours, was one of the most enchanting I have ever taken."

Just before reaching Spello, near a water fountain you will come to another devotional Marian shrine, known as Maestà di Mascione, full of candles, flowers, and photos of loved ones. There are some park benches nearby. This is a good place to sit for a few minutes and drink from the fountain and pray or meditate. Roadside devotional shrines, like this one, are ubiquitous along Italy's country roads; they are a popular form of devotion among country people.

Soon, you will enter Spello through the Porta Montanara gate. The town is well worth a visit for the churches containing lovely works of art (though the churches close mid-day).

After reaching Spello, continue the next six kilometers through residential neighborhoods to Foligno. If you prefer to take it easy, you could consider taking the train, as there is frequent service and the ride takes about seven or eight minutes. (See Stage 1a, for more information on walking to Foligno.)

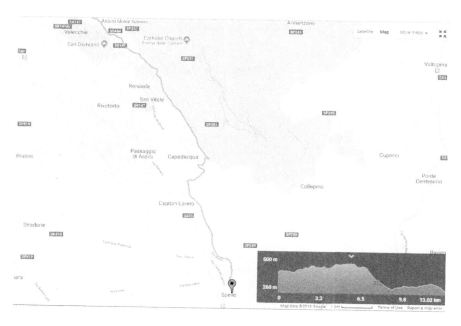

(NB: Map is Assisi to Spello)

Stage 1a: Assisi to Foligno (harder route)
Distance: 22 kilometers
Cumulative increase in altitude: + 925 m
Cumulative loss of altitude: - 1034 m
Surface: asphalt, gravel, dirt trails
Time: 8 hours
Difficulty: Very Difficult
Relive Video: relive.cc/view/v36ArpRzYZq

There in the clefts of the rock he would build his nest and in the hollow places of the wall his dwelling [...] He frequently chose solitary places so that he could direct his mind completely to God.
(Thomas of Celano, *First Life*, Chapter 27, 71)

Daily Franciscan Spirituality/reflection: Prayer

- *(If you walk the easier route to Foligno, use this reflection on prayer on another day.)*
- Prayer was at the heart of the life of Francis. Francis would spend upwards of four or five months, each year, in the mountain hermitages (like the Carceri) throughout central Italy.
- While we hear a lot about the things St. Francis said and did, we typically do not emphasize enough the contemplative aspect of Franciscan spirituality. Before Francis engaged in active service, he would pray fervently.
- Though very few of us have a full forty days to dedicate solely to prayer, Francis' attitude toward prayer can guide us in our own prayer life.
- Consider the importance of prayer to Francis and his spirituality.
- Reflect on how Francis' prayer life can guide your own.

Route notes:

- The harder route between Assisi and Foligno is a magnificent, though grueling, trek up and over Mount Subasio. Breathtaking views abound in all directions.
- There are several ways to get to Foligno on the harder route; the official Camino originally passed through the Carceri hermitage, at the end of which there was an open gate, but it is now closed.
- Further, the "official" St. Francis Camino route, as established by the region of Umbria, merged with a trail created by Camino enthusiast, Angela Seracchioli, in her Italian guidebook, "*On the Road with St. Francis*," published by Terre di Mezzo. This new "official" route makes the "hard route" even more difficult. All three variations are noted in the Route text below.

- Note also that some Guidebooks finish the first stage in Spello, while others continue to Foligno for overnight. You may wish to overnight in Spello, which would make the day's stage a little shorter.

<u>The Route:</u>

If you prefer to make today's "Very Difficult" stage a little less difficult, you could consider taking a taxi up to the Carceri hermitage and beginning there; this will eliminate a very long steep 400-meter climb out of the gates of Assisi up Mount Subasio.

Otherwise, begin in Assisi's upper square, Piazza Matteotti and follow the yellow/blue signs to the gate at the northern part of the square known as Porta Perlici. Exit the city gate and turn immediately right where a hiking trail begins and leads to the Rocca Minore (Assisi's Minor Castle). Alternatively, you could exit through the Porta Cappuccini gate (the gate uphill beyond the high schools on your right), pass through the gate, and turn immediately left on the dirt road to walk up to the Rocca Minore.

From the Rocca Minore, be prepared for a steep climb for the next 45 minutes as you climb 400 meters up the mountain. Follow yellow/blue markings and GPX tracks (noting that the trail coincides with a red/white CAI marking). Once the trail levels out, enjoy views of the valley as you begin to descend somewhat, then come out on a paved road; turn right and go slightly downhill toward the entrance gates of the Carceri hermitage by a parking lot and souvenir kiosk which you will not miss.

Note that if you would like a less strenuous walk — though also less scenic — you could consider walking up the paved road (through Porta Cappuccini in Piazza Matteotti) all the way to the Carceri hermitage. Many pilgrims do just that, mostly because they don't know about the trail.

After visiting the Carceri hermitage, return to the kiosk and go straight on the paved road back slightly uphill: in less than one meters, make a quick right turn on Via San Benedetto. As you follow the paved road, you will note that you are walking above the Carceri hermitage which you may be able to see on your right below you.

After passing the hermitage, you will see a yellow/blue sign pointing to a trail downhill to the right. If you follow this trail, it will bring you to the (now closed) gate at the rear of the Carceri hermitage; the trail then continues with a considerable downhill jaunt which eventually re-connects with the lower part of Via San Benedetto, the road you are now on, only to climb back uphill at a sharp bend in the road in a few kilometers in front of you. To make things easier, you can continue straight on the paved Via San Benedetto until you come to the sharp bend in two or so kilometers.

As you continue walking on Via San Benedetto, in several hundred meters after the sign pointing to your right, you may notice another yellow/blue sign pointing up the mountain on your left. This is the most recent modification to the official trail when it merged with a different Camino — that of Angela Seracchioli. If you turn left here, you will climb an additional 500 meters sea level to an altitude above the tree line of Mt. Subasio. Though it will certainly afford some spectacular views of the Spoleto Valley, it will also make for a very challenging day's hike. If you go left up the mountain, the trail is somewhat well-marked with yellow/blue signs, but most GPX tracks cover the older trail.

Otherwise, continue walking straight on Via San Benedetto until you come to a sharp bend in the road. You will see yellow/blue signs, as well as other red and white CAI trail markers, indicating to turn into the woods to your left.

Note that you may wish to continue downhill on the paved road, where in about five hundred meters you will arrive at the ruined, though somewhat restored, fenced monastery of San Benedetto on your left. This was a thriving monastery in Francis' era and in fact the Abbot here gave permission to Francis to take up residence at their property of St. Mary of the Angels. Today there is a small community of contemporary monks seeking to reestablish a residence.

From the bend in the road, enter the woods on the marked dirt trail. Shortly after turning off the paved road, you will pass two cliffs on your right; the first requires a scramble but is worth it for the selfie shot with the Spoleto valley in the background. About 100 meters down the trail you will come to "Sasso Rosso" (Red Rock). Nearby are the ruins of a castle once owned by the Scifi clan, Clare's father and uncle, and where she took refuge with her family during the civil war of Assisi in 1299. Sasso Rosso is a good place for a lunch or snack break.

From Sasso Rosso, continue following the yellow/blue signs all the way to Spello. As you descend the south side of Mt. Subasio, some magnificent views of the Spoleto valley begin to open up. There are also some nice views of Spello in front of you.

Just before you arrive at the old gates in upper Spello, there is a well-preserved ancient Roman aqueduct on your left and right. If you still have the energy, you can walk the length of the aqueduct, about three kilometers (each way).

Soon, you will enter Spello through the Porta Montanara gate. The town is well worth a visit for the churches containing lovely works of art (though the churches close mid-day).

The next jaunt — from Spello to Foligno — is mostly through paved suburban streets. (If you prefer a break, you could consider taking a train, which departs frequently and takes only about seven or eight minutes.) If you walk to Foligno, exercise caution when you cross and walk along Viale Firenze, as it is a main thoroughfare. Continue towards Foligno and cross the bridge over the Topino River. Just beyond the bridge, to the left, is the little church of San Giacomo: here you may wish to go in and visit the church (if it is open), as it is dedicated to the patron saint of pilgrims — San Giacomo (St. James). Next, veer to the right and walk on Via Venti Settembre towards Foligno's central square, Piazza della Repubblica.

Franciscan places on the route:

Assisi: Basilica of St. Francis, Basilica of St. Clare, Hermitage of the Carceri, Sanctuary of San Damiano, Basilica of St. Mary of the Angels, Chiesa Nuova and oratory of San Francesco Piccolino, house of Bernard of Quintavalle, Church of Santa Maria Maggiore and the Vescovado bishop's palace, Cathedral of San Rufino, San Quirico Poor Clare monastery (great place to join sisters for liturgy), Abbey of San Benedetto on Mt. Subasio (ruined), Bosco of San Francesco, Basilica of Rivotorto, leper church of Santa Maria Maddalena.

Spello: Church and convent of San Girolamo, Church of Sant'Andrea Apostolo, Church and monastery of Santa Maria di Vallegloria

Other places of interest:

Assisi: Minor and Major Rocca castles, churches of Santo Stefano and Minerva, Roman Forum museum, Benedictine Abbey of San Pietro

Spello: the church of Santa Maria Maggiore containing the Baglioni chapel and frescoes from Perugino and Pinturicchio, the church of San Lorenzo.

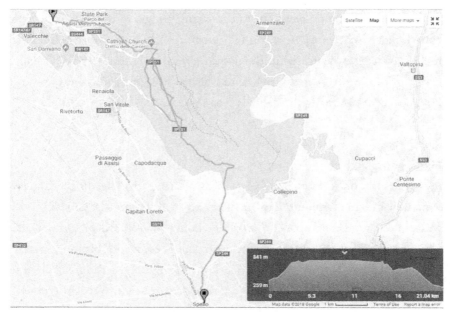

(NB: Map is Assisi to Spello)

Stage 2: From Foligno to Trevi
Distance: 13 kilometers
Cumulative increase in altitude: + 425 m
Cumulative loss of altitude: - 240 m
Surface: asphalt road, gravel roads
Time: 6 hours
Difficulty: Moderate
Relive Video: relive.cc/view/vYvE9PnNZwv

He arose therefore, fortifying himself by the sign of the holy Cross, prepared his horse, mounted, and taking with him scarlet cloths to sell, came in haste to the city called Foligno. Here, having as usual sold all the goods he brought, the happy merchant left behind the horse he was riding, after receiving its price.
(Thomas of Celano, *First Life*, 333-335)

<u>Daily Franciscan Spirituality/reflection: Poverty</u>

- During Francis' life, there was a large marketplace in Foligno; it was here where he sold his father's cloth and horse in order to rebuild the ruined church of San Damiano. Later, Francis was called to give away everything and follow God in complete poverty.
- Poverty begins with complete surrender of ourselves to God; indeed all Christian spirituality, begins with the recognition of the primacy of God – the belief that God is primary, preeminent, and foundational in our lives.
- What do you think about the choices of poverty made by Francis?
- Though few of us are called to live exactly like Francis, can his example lead us to make changes in our own life?

<u>Route notes:</u>

- Today's walk from the memorable Roman/medieval city of Foligno involves a gradual climb from the valley up to Trevi.
- Pleasant views of the Spoleto valley through Umbria's legendary terraced olive groves, all the while in the shadow of the Apennine Mountains.
- Foligno to Trevi is considerably shorter than yesterday's trek and offers a gentle respite
- Take some time to explore Foligno before setting out, as well as Trevi upon arrival.

<u>The Route:</u>

Before leaving Foligno, make sure you visit the Duomo, containing the remains of the ancient martyr/bishop, Saint Feliciano, patron of Foligno. (Note that it is closed, at time of printing, due to earthquake damage). Note also in the square, on the side of one of the buildings, a plaque commemorating this square as the site where Francis sold his father's cloth and horse to rebuild the little church of San Damiano in Assisi.

On your way out of town, not far from the cathedral, and just a block or so off the Camino path, don't skip the Franciscan church housing the relics of St. Angela of Foligno. (Note that the main church is closed. However, the relics of St. Angela, in addition to a number of early Franciscan martyrs, are conserved in the side chapel which is open except at mid-day.)

Now make your way out of the center of Foligno through Porta Romana city gate and walk along Corso Cavour. (Note Foligno's train station, a major railway hub, is on your left here if you need public transport). Continue walking along the sidewalk all the way to the charming walled village of Sant'Eraclio. After a few minutes poking around (and filling up your water bottles or having a snack), veer left toward the foothills, pass under the state highway, and begin a slight uphill climb into the charming Umbrian countryside.

As you walk along lightly trafficked gravel and paved roads, enjoy the land replete with olive groves. Pass above the small town of Matigge and the outskirts of Santa Maria in Valle where you may wish to get a snack and replenish your water supplies. From the small church of Santa Maria in Valle, enjoy the scenic views of the Umbrian Valley. After the area of San Clemente, begin your final ascent into the old center of Trevi.

As you look back, you can see Mt. Subasio with Assisi on its northern spur and appreciate the distance you have already covered.

As you enter Trevi, on your right, across from the war memorial, there is a café bar with outdoor seating, which seems like it was put there to welcome weary pilgrims as they come into town. If you're craving American fare, they have hamburgers and hot dogs.

While in Trevi, make sure you sample something seasoned with its famous DOP olive oil that Trevi, and the area, is renowned for.

Franciscan places on the route:
Foligno: Sanctuary of Saint Angela of Foligno (also known as the Conventual Franciscan church of San Francesco): here you can visit the tomb of St. Angela as well as early Franciscan martyrs.

Trevi: The Poor Clare community of San Martino (about 1.5 kilometers north of center of Trevi) enjoy receiving pilgrims: you may wish to join them for liturgy; Church of San Francesco.

Other places of interest:
Foligno: Palazzo Trinci, cathedral housing the remains of the early bishop-martyr, San Feliciano (*currently closed due to earthquake damage*)
Trevi: Abbey of San Pietro in Bovara, Church of Madonna di Pietra Rossa, in lower Trevi is the Church of Madonna delle Lacrime (Our Lady of Tears) — or you can visit Madonna delle Lacrime the following day as the Camino passes nearby it on the way out of town; it boasts frescoes by Perugino and dello Spagna; San Francesco Museum Complex housing the art collection of San Francesco and the Olive Oil Museum; Piazza Mazzini with municipality and medieval tower; Teatro Clitunno opera house.

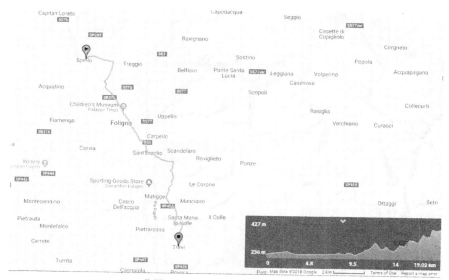

(NB: Map is Spello to Trevi)

Stage 3: From Trevi to Poreta
Distance: 12 kilometers
Cumulative increase in altitude: + 410 m
Cumulative loss of altitude: - 430 m
Surface: asphalt road, gravel roads
Time: 5 hours
Difficulty: Difficult
Relive Video: relive.cc/view/vr63ZxgV48O

[In Trevi], blessed Francis before everyone said to him: "Brother donkey, be quiet and let me preach". And here the donkey immediately calmed down, put his head between his paws and remained silent.
(*De Conformitate*, Bartholomew of Pisa)

Daily Franciscan Spirituality/reflection: Humility

- By now you have come to appreciate Italy's topography: its mountainous terrain, rolling hills, and valleys indeed create some spectacular scenery and vistas (and make for tough walking). But it adds another dimension to Franciscan spirituality: humility.

- When you look around, you'll notice that seemingly on the highest hills, mountains, or knolls is a monastery or palace. This was not just for security, as the ancient people believed that the higher one was, the more "noble" one was.
- This gives meaning to Francis' choice to leave upper Assisi for the valleys and the plains since the lower areas were near the lepers and poor people. This was the choice of "minority" or lesserness; for Francis, it was a geographic choice as much as spiritual.
- To be "minor," or "lesser," is to embrace poverty, humility, meekness, gentleness, simplicity, trust, and obedience.
- What does humility mean to you? What are some ways you embrace humility?

Route notes:

- A quiet walk through olive groves and open countryside, past hermitages, country churches and walled villages, with views of Spoleto valley, dotted with tiny villages and hermitages.
- While some guidebooks deviate from the official Camino by combining two stages and going from Trevi all the way to Spoleto walking in the valley on a bike path, the official Umbrian Camino overnights in Poreta making for two stages to Spoleto.
- Poreta is a very small town with just one very small bar/grocery store; so, you should consider your needs for lunch or dinner before departing Trevi, as there are little to no options for meals in Poreta.
- As today's stage is not very long, take your time and enjoy the scenery.

The Route:

Today's Camino begins with a downhill jaunt from Trevi to the plain near the Monastery of the Madonna delle Lacrime, which is well worth a visit if it's open, and then over a paved road that leads to the panoramic trail. (Note that when you come to the road, Località la Croce Bovara, you should veer to the left if you are going towards Poreta, or right if you're following "*The Way of Francis*" guidebook to the bike path direct to Spoleto.)

After passing the non-descript town of Alvanischio, begin ascending through steep slopes of olive groves. Take some time to appreciate how the local people engineered terraced plots to make for better irrigation and easier olive cultivation.

In a while, you will pass by a Franciscan hermitage (once visited by Sts. Francis and Bernardine of Siena), known today as the *Eremo delle Allodole* hermitage. Founded in 1930 by Sister Maria, there are some sisters who still live a monastic life in the hermitage today. And while they are known to receive pilgrims, please be respectful of their space and time.

After a steep downhill jaunt, you'll begin making your way towards the fortified castle town of Campello Alto, whose white walls stand out in the landscape (though slightly off the main Camino trail). After another five kilometers, you will reach the very small town of Lenano, where you can fill up your water bottles. After you get back on the trail, you will pass numerous votive shrines devoted to the Virgin Mary; these are good places to stop for Marian devotion. From Lenano, there is just a little over two kilometers of mostly downhill walking all the way into Poreta.

If you still have some energy when you arrive at Poreta, consider climbing up to the top of the castle of Poreta; or you could wait for the next day as it is an option for leaving town.

Other places of interest:

Poreta: the castle of Poreta, olive museum (part of Terre di Poreta agritourism properties), town church, (Borgo della Marmotta and Villa della Genga are luxury agritourism properties with pools and spa facilities if you're willing to splurge).

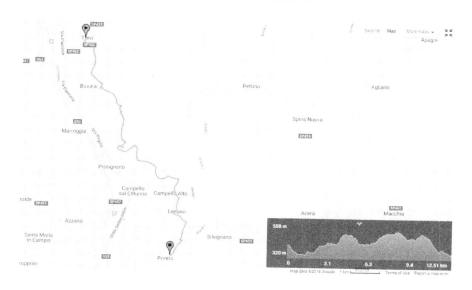

Stage 4: From Poreta to Spoleto
Distance: 15 kilometers
Cumulative increase in altitude: + 520 m
Cumulative loss of altitude: - 500 m
Surface: asphalt road, gravel roads
Time: 5 hours
Difficulty: Difficult
Relive Video: relive.cc/view/vLqeNV2MAdv

As he rode on his way and had already reached Spoleto, he began to feel somewhat dejected. Nevertheless, he was most eager to continue his journey, but when he lay down and was half asleep, he heard someone asking him whither he intended to go. After Francis had explained his plans, the voice said: "Who can help you more, the master or the man?" "The master," he replied. Again, the voice spoke, saying: "Why then do you forsake the master for the man, the Prince for the vassal?" And Francis said: "Lord, what should I do?" "Return to your home, and you will be told what you are to do. You must interpret the vision you had in your dream in a different way."
(*Legend of the Three Companions*, chapter Two)

Daily Franciscan Spirituality/reflection: Obedience

- St. Bonaventure wrote that Francis became obedient to God after this experience in Spoleto. In fact, that night Francis heard God speak, listened, and followed his command (the Latin root of the word "obey" derives etymologically from the word "listen").
- Where are you today in your faith journey? Ask yourself the question posed to Francis, "Who can do more for you, the Lord or his servant, a rich man or a beggar?" Ask yourself if you are serving the true Lord. If not, who is the servant in your life?
- Take a moment and look back at the times when you became aware of the presence of God and sought to follow him. Were you a child or an adult? Was your conversion in small steps, or was it dramatic – like St. Francis's?

Route notes:

- Today's walk continues through terraced olive groves concluding in Spoleto, one of Umbria's loveliest cities renowned not only for culture and art, but also forever memorialized in the story of St. Francis, as it is the site of his conversion.
- In Spoleto, Francis renounced his dreams of knighthood and returned to Assisi as a pauper.
- Preserved within a chapel inside the Duomo (cathedral) of Spoleto is a letter written by Francis' own hand.

The Route:

The Camino towards Spoleto begins with a few climbs followed by mostly downhill or flat walking. If you are up for a steep climb to get warmed up for the day, you can begin today's stage by climbing up to the old castle. Or, if you prefer to avoid the climb, walk south along Poreta's "main road" passing the church on your left and the coffee bar/grocery store on your right, and make your first left on Frazione Poreta (roughly 200 meters past the coffee bar), then, in another 300 meters, go right still on Frazione Poreta to rejoin the trail; there are yellow/blue signs if you choose to go up to the castle or stay on the low road.

If you go up to the castle, as you skirt the ancient walls, you'll reach an area where you can drink from a water fountain next to a votive shrine. A narrow trail then passes through the woods to the area known locally as Località Osteria ("Inn Locality") which would indicate that there was once an inn for travelers or pilgrims here.

After a brief flat walk, you'll begin a climb through a shady area with plenty of vegetation. After about five kilometers from Poreta, you will arrive in the area of Bazzano Superiore, where you can take a break and refill your water underneath the pine trees in front of the church. From here to Spoleto, much of your journey is downhill or flat (with the exception of one uphill between lower Bazzano and Eggi), starting with a descending trail through the woods.

As you pass through the castle town of Eggi, go inside the church of San Giovanni Battista (hopefully it is open) where the apse is decorated with frescoes painted by Spaniard painter, Lo Spagna, during the High Renaissance. Note that the church of San Michele Arcangelo, located before San Giovanni Battista, is also beautifully frescoed and merits a visit as well.

As you make your way into the outskirts of Spoleto, don't miss the Romanesque, Lombard-era, ninth-century Basilica of San Salvatore, a UNESCO world heritage site since 2011. Though the church is closed due to the earthquake, the façade warrants a visit in and of itself. By now you'll be able to admire Spoleto's impressive "Rocca" (fortress) dominating the skyline.

Once in Spoleto, I suggest you spend some time walking through the old center to appreciate its tremendous religious and cultural legacy. Spoleto is an internationally renowned city for cultural events; it hosts the "Festival of the Two Worlds" in July, and there are also art festivals in the US borrowing the city's name.

In the life of St. Francis, Spoleto played an important part in his conversion: Francis was overnighting in Spoleto on his way to fight in the Crusades. Yet, here he had a dream in which he heard a voice asking him if it were better to serve the Lord or the servant. The next morning, he left his armor and horse and walked back to Assisi and dedicated himself to a life of penance and poverty.

Spoleto is the last sizable city until you get to Rieti.

Franciscan places on the route:
Spoleto: Cathedral with letter written by St. Francis to Brother Leo, just one of two existing documents written by Francis' own hand; Franciscan hermitage of Monteluco.

Other places of interest:
Spoleto: the church of San Salvatore, UNESCO heritage site, at the entrance to town; cathedral (duomo) with its mosaic facade, Cosmatesque floor, frescoed apse, and altar cross; Ponte delle Torri "Bridge of Towers" (although closed to foot traffic due to earthquake); Rocca Albornoziana fortress including National Museum of Duchy of Spoleto; Church of San Sabino.

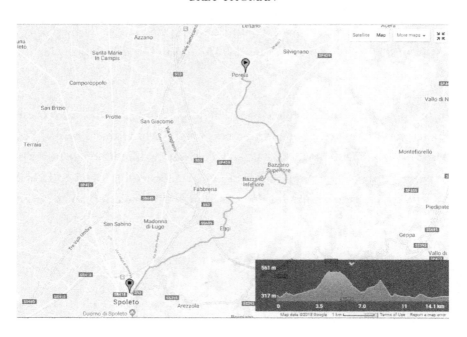

Stage 5: From Spoleto to Ceselli

Distance: 17 kilometers
Cumulative increase in altitude: + 641 m
Cumulative loss of altitude: - 663 m
Surface: dirt trails, gravel roads, asphalt roads
Time: 7 hours
Difficulty: Experts Only
Relive Video: relive.cc/view/vYvE9P5LGwv

Daily Franciscan Spirituality/reflection: Penance

- Francis devoted himself to penance as a way of life and referred to it frequently in his writings. The word penance, however, has various meanings: it can mean denying one's self pleasures; inflicting corporal disciplines; it recalls the sacrament also referred to as "confession"; it is also the penalty for sins.

- Yet, penance is any voluntarily chosen action to grow closer to God by increasing virtue and avoiding vice.

- Francis believed that by practicing specific actions, he could convert more fully. Thus, he embraced ascetic practices, solitary prayer, giving alms, going on pilgrimages, re-building churches, and perhaps more fundamentally, serving lepers. These were all his penances.

- Yet, for Francis, penance meant "conversion."
- Number 1435 of the Catechism of the Catholic Church says: "Conversion is accomplished in daily life by gestures of reconciliation, concern for the poor, the exercise and defense of justice and right, by the admission of faults to one's brethren, fraternal correction, revision of life, examination of conscience, spiritual direction, acceptance of suffering, endurance of persecution for the sake of righteousness. Taking up one's cross each day and following Jesus is the surest way of penance."
- What are some penitential actions you already take, or can take, in order to grow closer to God?

Route notes:

- Today's stage is one of the most difficult on the entire Camino, as it involves some steep climbs and descents up and over the Apennine Mountains as you move from the Spoleto Valley into the Nera Valley.
- But your physical exertion will be rewarded by the scenery and places along the way: the Ponte delle Torri bridge, the spirituality of the hermitage of Monteluco, and vistas of the mountains, gorges and the Nera River valley, known as the Valnerina.
- Note that the Ponte delle Torri bridge is closed due to earthquake damage; the route notes below offer two alternate routes.
- Exercise caution today: only attempt this stage if you are in good physical shape and the trail is dry. The stage begins with a 500-meter climb up to the hermitage of Monteluco followed by another 200-meter climb arriving almost at the summit; this is followed by a steep descent on the other side into the Nera Valley that can be treacherous when wet.

- After the hermitage of Monteluco, you will be in the remote wilderness until reaching Pontuglia on the other side; there are pockets where there is no cell phone coverage.
- There are few accommodations in Ceselli (only a "community center"); many prefer to continue another five kilometers to Macenano where there are some better accommodations.
- Make sure you bring a lot of water, snacks, and allow yourself plenty of time (water is available in Spoleto, Monteluco and in Pontuglia).
- Note also that sundown arrives earlier in the mountains, which can come uncomfortably early in the cold months.
- The Ponte delle Torri bridge is currently closed due to earthquake precaution rendering the route up to Monteluco rather circuitous.

<u>The Route:</u>

If you're beginning from a hotel in lower Spoleto, there are escalators that will aid in your climb up to the duomo (cathedral) which you can explore before beginning your walk. Of interest are its mosaic facade, Cosmatesque floor, frescoed apse, and altar cross, as well as letter written by St. Francis to Brother Leo.

After visiting the cathedral, you may wish to go up to the fortress (Albornoziana Rocca) which you can explore. Make sure to view the belvedere, where there is a stone with the inscription of the phrase attributed to St. Francis, *"Nil iucundius vidi valle mea spoletana"* ("I've never seen anything more cheerful than my Spoleto Valley").

Ordinarily you would now head over toward the medieval aqueduct (Roman in origin but from the fourteenth century in its present form) to begin your climb up to Monteluco. However, the earthquakes of 2016 have led to it being closed indefinitely out of precaution. Therefore, you will probably have to take a detour around the bridge. You have two options.

The first is by walking out of the old part of Spoleto, south, and cross the busy highway, SS3, in front of the basilica of San Pietro. Exercise extreme caution here as Italian drivers are notorious for driving excessively fast. Then walk on the windy paved road until you reach the trail on the southeastern side of the Ponte delle Torri bridge. (Note that this detour adds about 2 kilometers and 30 minutes to today's walk).

Otherwise, you can avoid crossing the busy highway and spend more time walking in the quiet mountains. From Spoleto's cathedral, go down the flight of stairs adjacent to the bell tower and then down more stairs on Via delle Mura Ciclopiche. At the bottom of the stairs, turn right on Via Ponziana, in a few meters, keep right, remaining on Via Ponziana, and soon you will exit the walled town. Walk across the bridge and then turn right on Via del Tiro a Segno, following the sign, "tiro a segno nazionale", and soon you will pass beneath the busy highway. Continue straight until you reach the yellow sign, "TIRO A SEGNO NAZ – POLIGONO DI TIRO" (roughly 300 meters from the Spoleto walls). Turn right, cross a small bridge, then make a quick left to enter the trailhead. Pass the church of Santa Elisabetta and 500 meters from the beginning of the trailhead, you will arrive at an intersection. Turn right and follow this trail, known as the Giro dei Condotti. Pass the Grotta degli Affreschi (frescoed cave), and in roughly one kilometer from your righthand turn, you will arrive at the southeastern side of the closed Ponte delle Torri bridge. Here you can pick up the original Camino trail and follow the yellow/blue signs up to Monteluco.

Though a demanding climb up switchbacks to the "*Sacro Bosco*" (Sacred Woods) of Monteluco, the dense forest of seemingly timeless, almost mystical, helm oaks (ilex trees) seems to generate energy.

Once at Monteluco, take some time to explore the environs. Monteluco is known locally as the Mt. Athos of Umbria for its spirituality and is considered the sister mountain in the Spoleto Valley with Mt. Subasio for its spirituality.

The Romans believed the forest to be sacred, so much that they forbade the cutting of the trees or otherwise damaging the forest (the punishments were coded in a stone tablet still in the forest). Make sure you walk around the forest and find the grottos where St. Anthony prayed. This is a great spot for photos of the valley.

After Monteluco, there won't be much civilization other than a few houses and a gravel road until you get to Pontuglia on the other side of the mountain.

Locate the yellow/blue signs and follow the trail which ascends another 150 meters or so in altitude. Not long before the summit, you will pass a white house; there are sometimes dogs here that may be meddlesome, so exercise caution.

When you reach the fork near Castel del Monte, the highest elevation on today's stage, you will arrive at a meadow which is a great place to stop for lunch or a snack. You'll also want to take in the extraordinary views of the gorge in the direction of the Nera Valley.

As you begin walking down towards the valley, you'll be mostly on wide paths, foot paths or secondary roads. At times, however, you are on narrower foot trails; note that footing may be slippery after heavy rains when there will be mud and runoff water. Also, you wind around a gorge and there are some steep drops, though not excessive, to the left.

After the crest, you will begin to discern a small town in the distance past the gorge below; that is Pontuglia, and you will soon be descending towards it and winding around to the right (south) of it. Make your way down through woods and past hidden hermitages towards the Nera river valley until you pass Pontuglia and then arrive in Ceselli.

In Ceselli (population of a few dozen), there is an overnight option in Casa Vacanze Il Ruscello with its adjacent restaurant/pizzeria that is not always open. Otherwise, if you continue to Macenano (five kilometers) — a long flat walk along the Nera River — there are more options for accommodations.

Franciscan places on the route:

Monteluco: A must-see Franciscan site is the hermitage of Monteluco, a 45-minute hike up the mountain behind Spoleto. Monteluco is considered one of two holy mountains in the Spoleto Valley (the other is Mt. Subasio). St. Francis himself spent time in prayer here (as did St. Bernardine of Siena, St. Anthony of Padua, and even Michelangelo who was a tertiary Franciscan). The ilex (holm oak) forest surrounding the hermitage offers striking views of the valley as well and contains grottoes in addition to a stone tablet from the Roman era declaring the forest sacred and decreeing fines if vandalized — the first recorded conservation laws known in the western world.

Other places of interest:

Ceselli: the tiny towns and settlements that dot the Nera Valley are known more for their natural beauty and nature parks than cultural attractions.

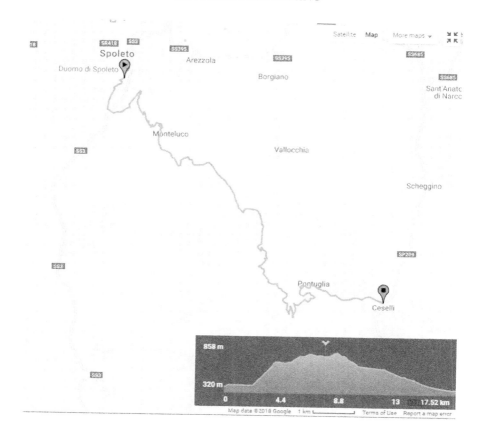

Stage 6: From Ceselli to Arrone
Distance: 16 kilometers
Cumulative increase in altitude: + 221 m
Cumulative loss of altitude: - 248 m
Surface: asphalt roads, gravel roads, dirt trails
Time: 5 hours
Difficulty: Easy
Relive Video: relive.cc/view/vDqgJVxnBG6

*Be praised, my Lord, through Sister Water; she is very useful,
and humble, and precious, and pure.*
(Saint Francis of Assisi, *Canticle of the Creatures*)

Daily Franciscan Spirituality/reflection: Creation

- St. Francis was declared the Patron Saint of Ecology in 1979 by St. John Paul II.
- While many people today enjoy being in nature and love the outdoors — hiking, camping, and riding bikes – Francis' understanding of creation was Christological at its root. It was incarnational, even sacramental: for Francis saw the reflection of Christ in all created things.
- This comes from Scripture: "All things came to be through him, and without him nothing came to be" (John 1: 2-3); "He is the image of the invisible God, the firstborn of all creation. For in him were created all things in heaven and on earth, the visible and the invisible." (Colossians 1: 15-20)
- With such a Christological worldview, it was natural for Francis to see Christ in all forms of creation. This is why he wrote his famed Canticle of the Creatures in which he referred to elements of nature — "Brother Sun" and "Sister Moon" — fraternally.
- Such a theological/fraternal understanding of creation naturally leads followers of Franciscan spirituality to desire to care for and be mindful of nature ecologically.
- Pope Francis, in his encyclical letter, *Laudato si'*, wrote of the importance of a renewed theological understanding between humanity and the care of the environment:
  - We are not God. The earth was here before us and it has been given to us. This allows us to respond to the charge that Judeo-Christian thinking, on the basis of the Genesis account which grants man "dominion" over the earth (cf. *Gen* 1:28), has encouraged the unbridled exploitation of nature by painting him as domineering and destructive by nature. This is not a correct interpretation of the Bible as understood by the Church. Although it is true that we Christians have at times incorrectly interpreted the Scriptures, nowadays we must forcefully reject the notion that our being created in God's image and given

dominion over the earth justifies absolute domination over other creatures. The biblical texts are to be read in their context, with an appropriate hermeneutic, recognizing that they tell us to "till and keep" the garden of the world (cf. *Gen* 2:15). "Tilling" refers to cultivating, ploughing or working, while "keeping" means caring, protecting, overseeing and preserving. This implies a relationship of mutual responsibility between human beings and nature. Each community can take from the bounty of the earth whatever it needs for subsistence, but it also has the duty to protect the earth and to ensure its fruitfulness for coming generations. [67]

- What are some practical ways you show fraternal respect for creation?

Route notes:

- Ceselli to Arrone is an easy, relatively flat, stroll along the cool, tree-shaded banks of the Nera River guarded over by evocative castles and walled hilltop towns. After yesterday's toil, today's 16 kilometers will be a welcome respite.
- According to a local legend, the Nera River valley (with its twists and turns) was infested by a dragon who was defeated by early Christian missionaries; after its defeat, it left its form on the valley.
- Since today's walk is fairly short, it may be worth a detour to visit the restored tenth-century Abbey of San Pietro in Valle, near Macenano, where the lovely abbey with its artwork can be visited (there are limited opening hours; entrance fee).

The Route:

From Ceselli, cross the highway and then a bridge over the Nera River to the east side of the river which you will flank all the way to your destination. As you walk along a lovely trail through the cultivated fields and forests of the

Nera River valley park, enjoy the scenery of the narrow valley surrounded by steep slopes and the gurgling sound of the river.

The first town you reach, Macenano, five kilometers from Ceselli (on the west side of the river from the trail), has a bar and restaurant (and hotel), Tre Archi, should you wish to stop and rest. Or you may wish to detour up to the abbey of San Pietro — though it is uphill and two kilometers each way. If you're overnighting in Macenano, enjoy the scrumptious dinner prepared with local fare by the Tre Archi proprietors; otherwise, you may wish to stop in for a gelato and cool beverage.

In another five kilometers you will pass between two more hill towns, Precetto and Ferrentillo (with castle), visible for some time on either side of the valley from the trail. Precetto, on the Camino, may be a good place to stop for a snack and fill up on water.

Finally, in another seven kilometers, you'll reach Arrone, an ancient village founded by the Romans. Its proximity to the famed Marmore waterfalls have turned this town into an important center for popular water sports like canoeing and kayaking. Take some time exploring its narrow alleys and steep streets up to the ancient part of town where you can visit what's left of the original eleventh-century castle and the church dedicated to St. John the Baptist.

Other places of interest:
Precetto: Museum of Mummies, church of Santo Stefano.
Arrone: Santa Maria Assunta (in the center of the lower, newer part of town); church of San Giovanni Battista (St. John the Baptist) — a gothic church with 15th-century frescoes (in the older/upper part of town); ex convent of St. Francis.

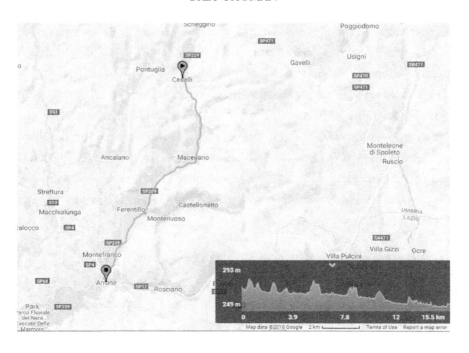

Stage 7: From Arrone to Piediluco
Distance: 14 kilometers
Cumulative increase in altitude: + 294 m
Cumulative loss of altitude: - 152 m
Surface: asphalt roads, gravel roads, dirt trails
Time: 4.5 hours
Difficulty: Moderate
Relive Video: relive.cc/view/vZqNN5EZ93q

Two men and two women, with a child, were sailing on the lake of Piediluco, when suddenly the boat capsized and filled with water, and the death of all on board seemed imminent. While everyone was screaming in fright, without any hope of being saved, one of the women shouted with great confidence: "Saint Francis, you who gave me the gift of friendship while alive, now bring help from heaven to us who are about to succumb." The invoked saint suddenly appeared and led the boat filled with water to shore in complete safety. (Thomas of Celano, *Treatises of Miracles,* chapter 10, 84)

Daily Franciscan Spirituality/reflection: Lepers

- Francis himself claimed that his penance (conversion) began when he encountered a leper: in 1226, two years before Francis died, he wrote in his Testament: "The Lord gave me, Brother Francis, thus to begin doing penance in this way: for when I was in sin, it seemed too bitter to me to see lepers. And the Lord Himself led me among them and I showed mercy to them. And when I left them, what had seemed bitter to me was turned into sweetness of soul and body. And afterward I delayed a little and left the world."

- His experience with the leper radically changed his worldview; it turned it upside down. While before this experience he wanted to become a knight, and go up in the world, after his conversion he sought the lowliest: the leper.

- After the experience embracing the leper, Francis visited the leper communities often and served them. He also required it of the young men who wished to join his Order.

- What must have happened to Francis so that he would be able to experience joy in embracing, greeting, and serving lepers?

- Who is the "leper" in your life? Can you find the courage to "embrace" that person?

Route notes:

- Today's walk is fairly easy except for one steep hike up to the Marmore waterfalls.

- Try to time your walk by the Cascate delle Marmore waterfalls (the highest falls in Europe, engineered in Roman times) when the falls are open, as it is an extraordinary sight.

The Route:

From Arrone, find the staircase behind the church of Santa Maria Assunta and work your way down past the sports field to the valley floor. Pick up the trail and you will soon rejoin the Nera River. In a few kilometers of flat walking along the Nera, you'll peel away from the river to the left and enter the wooded hill in front of you. Note that just before you begin the climb up to Marmore, there is a confusing fork: one sign says go right to Piediluco while the yellow/blue says to go left to Cascate Marmore; follow the YB to the left.

After a steep climb up some switchbacks, you'll be rewarded with the spectacular Cascate delle Marmore. The Marmore falls, at 165 meters, are the highest manmade waterfalls in Europe. In ancient Roman times, the Rieti Valley was a malaria-infested wetland caused by the overflowing Velino River. Therefore, the industrious Romans sought to drain the valley by channeling the water toward the cliff overlooking the Nera Valley thus creating the falls. In modern times, the falls have been converted into a source of electrical power, testified to by the turbines to your right as you enter the park. If the falls are open it's worth the reasonable ticket entrance to view the extraordinary beauty and awesome power of rushing water. Opening times vary, but are essentially when tourists are more likely to visit; that is, on the weekends in the off season and morning/afternoon daily during the summer (www.marmorefalls.it/ita/1/orari).

After exiting the environs of the falls, pass the parking lot and pick up the Camino. From the town of Marmore, follow the Velino River past the dam and reservoir until you reach Piediluco Lake.

When the trail reaches the lake (where you open and close a gate), exercise caution as the Camino temporarily merges with Highway 79 — a busy road that winds around the fingers of the lake with no shoulder to walk on. Note that there is a variation in the Camino allowing you to avoid most of the busy road by detouring you into the hills to the north of the lake.

On your way into town, stop in the church of St. Francis, today's parish church of Piediluco, marking the site where St. Francis preached and built a hut for his followers when he visited the town.

The town of Piediluco and its charming lake are your last overnight in Umbria before you arrive tomorrow in the region of Lazio's Holy Valley of Rieti. Spend some time overlooking the lake where perhaps you'll see some rowers, as Piediluco is the headquarters of the Italian national rowing team.

<u>Must-see:</u>

Piediluco:

- The sanctuary of San Francesco. Built at the end of the twelfth century, it was finished in 1338 in memory of St. Francis' visit here; it is the main parish church in town today.
- The remains of the church (circa 1000 AD), one of the most ancient Romanesque churches in the area.
- The church of Madonna della Maestà (from the beginning of the 16th century); near the old cemetery, it is still used for religious rites.

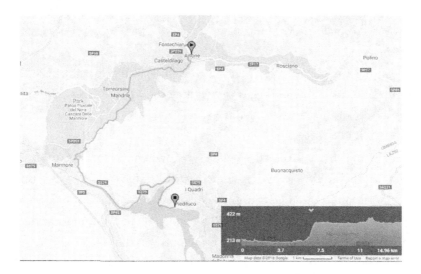

- The town at Poggio Bustone is famed for Francis' greeting to the locals saying: "*Buon giorno, Buona gente!*" (Good morning, good people!).
- Poggio Bustone is the first of the four famed Franciscan sanctuaries in the "Sacred" Rieti Valley; the others are: La Foresta, Greccio, and Fonte Colombo.
- The city of Poggio Bustone, population 2,000, is also known as the birthplace of famed Italian singer-songwriter, Lucio Battisti.

The Route:

With the lakeshore to your right, walk east and in the distance, you can see the small charming hill town of Labro, your first goal for the day. Pass the local rowing club of Piediluco and then a campsite. In a few hundred meters, turn left and when you reach the highway, turn right and walk about 500 meters (be vigilant in the traffic) until you reach a water fountain, where you turn left on a paved road, Valle Spoletina. This was an ancient customs outpost marking the border between the Papal States and the Kingdom of Naples. Follow the yellow/blue signs as the road turns to gravel, crosses a small bridge, then turns right as you make your way up the steep hill to Labro.

Take some time to explore the intriguing labyrinthine alleyways of Labro before continuing.

The Camino then continues through some small settlements, like La Croce and Alvano. In La Croce (eight kilometers from starting point), there is a tiny eatery that may be open. When you arrive at a wooden cross, you'll see the first signs for "Faggio di San Francesco" (Beech Tree of St. Francis). After La Croce, the serious climbing through the remote part of today's stage begins in earnest.

When you finally arrive at the "Faggio," take some deserved rest in the truly majestic forest of beeches. There is a pilgrim's stamp chained to a table you can put in your *Credenziale*. After some reflection time underneath the branches that sheltered St. Francis during a storm, go back to the cross and begin your downhill descent into the valley.

Once you arrive in the town of Cepparo, where there is a water fountain, continue on the dirt road until you arrive in Poggio Bustone from the west. ("*Poggio*" means "knoll" or "hill" in Italian, and there are many towns with it in the name; it derives from the Latin word, *podium*, which we use in English for the small structure that elevates performers in public spaces.)

Make your way through town until you reach the sanctuary of St. Francis commemorating the episode from Francis' life when he helped people discover their inner goodness with the phrase, "*Buon giorno, buona gente*," (Good morning, good people). If you still have the energy for another steep 30-minute climb, you may consider climbing up to the secluded chapel and cave of Sacro Speco where Francis felt the love of God through the archangel, Gabriel.

Franciscan places on the route:

- Faggio Beech Tree: according to a local legend, Francis was in the area of Rivodutri when a heavy storm came through the area; Francis took refuge underneath the tree that held out its branches acting like an umbrella. (reflection on storm)
- Poggio Bustone: The Franciscan sanctuary of San Giacomo, above the city recalls the episode when Francis said, "*Buon giorno, buona gente*" ("Good morning, good people") to the local townspeople.
- Sacro Speco: a thirty-minute climb above the sanctuary in the mountains is a cave known as where Francis felt God's forgiveness of all his sins through the archangel, Gabriel.

Other places of interest:

- Labro: take some time to visit the medieval walled city of Labro, built in the tenth century; visit the castle and two towers, the church of Santa Maria Maggiore (with chapel of the Rosary).

Stage 9: From Poggio Bustone to Rieti
Distance: 18 kilometers
Cumulative increase in altitude: + 395 m
Cumulative loss of altitude: - 745 m
Surface: asphalt road, gravel roads, dirt paths
Time: 7 hours
Difficulty: Moderate
Relive Video: relive.cc/view/vYvrDm1K7L6

Blessed Francis at that time was staying in the church of San Fabiano [today the hermitage of La Foresta] near the same city [Rieti], where there was a poor secular priest. [...] That church had a small vineyard next to the house where blessed Francis was staying. There was one door to the house through which nearly all those who visited him passed into the vineyard, especially because the grapes were ripe at that time, and the place was pleasant for resting. And it came about that for that reason almost the entire vineyard was ruined. [...] The priest began to be offended and upset. "I lost my vintage for this year!" [...] "Don't be sad over this anymore," blessed Francis told him [...] And it happened that he obtained twenty measures and no less, just as blessed Francis had told him. (Assisi Compilation, 67)

Felix) (1515-1587), the first Capuchin Franciscan friar to be declared a saint. Of peasant origins, Felix entered the Capuchin Order and was sent to Rome where he was assigned to beg for the Order. He was known for his humility and graciousness as well as for working miracles. Hopefully the church will be open for a quick visit and prayer.

From Cantalice, look to the east for gorgeous views of Mt. Terminillo and west over the Rieti Valley where you can see lakes of Lungo and Ripasottile. In roughly three kilometers you will come to a peach-colored church. This is the sanctuary of *San Felice all'Acqua* (St. Felix at the Water). Open the gate and behind the church you will find a fountain and an explanation of a local legend (in Italian) about St. Felix. It says that when he was still a farmhand, Felix prayed to God for his companions who were toiling under the hot sun with nothing to drink; he struck the ground with his staff and a spring of water gurgled up. Feel free to drink and even fill up your water bottle from the same spring.

Exit the church, turn right, and continue downhill along a rocky path past a pen with farm animals. Walking through the bucolic Rieti countryside can be a step back in time as you'll occasionally happen on locals engaged in centuries-old professions like shepherding and small-scale farming.

In less than three kilometers, you will begin your final switchback up through the woods before arriving at the Franciscan sanctuary of Santa Maria della Foresta, or, more simply, La Foresta. For many centuries home to Franciscan friars, La Foresta now houses a community of young men recovering from drug and alcohol addiction, known as Mondo X. The church is always open and can be visited during any time of the day. For access inside the cloister, ring the bell. One of the community members welcomes pilgrims, though not during the mid-day rest period. If you can get inside, you will get to visit a cave where Francis prayed, as well as the house where he stayed while in Rieti for his eye operation and which houses the ancient wine press used during the miracle of the grapes.

BRET THOMAN

Now follow the Camino through the parking lot and walk the last four
kilometers through the suburban outskirts of Rieti until you reach your
overnight accommodations.

Rieti, population 48,000, is a delightful city known for history, culture and
culinary specialties (make sure you try the maltagliata pasta, or pasta alla gricia
or amatriciana).

In pre-Roman times, Rieti was the capital of the Sabine region and was
eventually appropriated into the expanding Roman Kingdom and eventual
Empire (the "Rape of the Sabine women" was part of the process). The
Romans built a road, the Via Salaria (Salt Way), that ran directly through
Rieti connecting Rome on the Tyrrhenian Sea to the shallower Adriatic Sea
in order to mine and transport salt. Today much of the historic part of Rieti
is preserved, though it suffered serious damage during World War II from
Allied aerial bombardment.

If you have time, visit the Church of St. Francis on the banks of the Velino
River to the east of the Roman bridge. In medieval times, the area was the site
of the leper hospital and was thus where the friars established their community
and church. Artistically, it boasts some frescoes from the school of Giotto.

Just off the main square in upper Rieti is the cathedral complex which is also
worth a visit. Adjacent is the papal residence where Pope Honorius III — one
of the pontiffs instrumental in the life of Francis and who approved his Rule
in 1223 — frequently sojourned.

Franciscan places on the route:

- Cantalice: church of San Felice (though often closed); three kilometers
  past Cantalice: sanctuary of miracle of water.

- La Foresta (five kilometers before arriving in Rieti): ring the bell and ask the porter to show you the ancient house in the courtyard where Francis recovered from eye surgery and where the miracle of the wine took place.
    - According to legend, in 1225, Francis came to Rieti for his eye surgery; in an effort to avoid the huge crowds, he took refuge outside the city in a house behind the church of San Fabiano here. Nonetheless, crowds came and trampled the vineyard which was the only source of revenue for the poor priest; Francis prayed and the few grapes remaining yielded a huge amount of wine.
    - There is also a cave behind the courtyard where Francis used to pray.
- Rieti:
    - Church of St. Francis

Other places of interest:

- Rieti:
    - Duomo/Cathedral and papal palace where Pope Honorius III frequently stayed.
    - Tour of Underground Rieti. Contact Rita Giovanelli (tel: 347 727 9591) for an impressive visit of the history of the city from beneath its roads and buildings. She begins in Roman history when Rieti was the central stopover point on the ancient Via Salaria to more recent times when Rieti became an important source of water (visit: www.rietidascoprire.it).
    - Roman bridge and Roman city gate: from Via Roma (once the Via Salaria) crossing the Velino River, look below you, to the east, and you will see the ancient Roman bridge that crossed the river on the ancient Via Salaria; continuing south a few hundred meters and you will come to the ancient city gate, the Porta Romana.

- Center of Italy square (Rieti boasts geographical center of Italy); a large travertine stone disc in Piazza Centro d'Italia marks the mathematical spot.

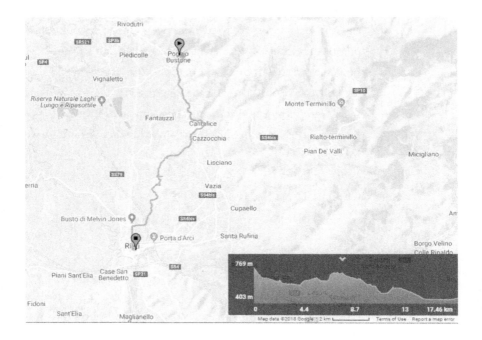

<u>Stage 9a: From Rieti to Greccio (*optional excursion*)</u>
Distance: 24 kilometers
Cumulative increase in altitude: + 470 m
Cumulative loss of altitude: - 390 m
Surface: asphalt roads, gravel roads, dirt trails, country roads
Time: 7.5 hours
Difficulty: Difficult
Relive Video: relive.cc/view/vZqNN5oVE3q

*Francis loved the hermitage of Greccio, where the friars were virtuous and poor,
and he also had a predilection for the inhabitants of that land for their poverty
and simplicity. For these reasons, he often went to rest and stay there, attracted
also by an extremely poor and isolated cell, where the holy father loved to gather
himself.* (*Legend of Perugia*, 34)

<u>Daily Franciscan Spirituality/reflection: Incarnation</u>

- Thomas of Celano said of Francis: "His highest aim, foremost desire,
  and greatest intention was to pay heed to the holy gospel in all things
  and through all things, to follow the teaching of our Lord Jesus Christ

and to retrace His footsteps completely with all vigilance and all zeal, all the desire of his soul and all the fervor of his heart."

- He desired greatly to reflect on and re-live the historical, concrete, human dimensions of the life of Christ – in Greccio, his birth.
- Through the nativity scene, Francis created the possibility of entering into the event. Through the presence of the characters – Mary, Joseph, the shepherds, the Magi, and the Christ-child himself – together with the animals, the hay, the manger, Francis enhanced the possibility of entering into the mystery of the Incarnation.
- The birth of Christ shows us the humility of God; that God did not become incarnate as a powerful prince or lord, rather as a poor child born in a manger, to poor parents.
- Reflect on how the Nativity, the Birth of Christ, teaches us about God: how God is humble, poor, nonviolent, and simple.

Route notes:

- Consider staying an extra night in Rieti in order to visit the hermitages of Fonte Colombo and Greccio — the site of the first nativity scene. By completing this stage, you will have visited all four Franciscan hermitages in the "Sacred Valley" of Rieti.
- In Fonte Colombo, Francis wrote his Rule in 1223, approved by the Pope.
- Greccio is the most well-known sanctuary in the Rieti Valley, as it is the site of the first ever live nativity scene, or crèche, begun by St. Francis in 1223.
- Today's stage is not particularly difficult, but the distance and hills make for a long day.
- There is a train station in the plains below the Greccio hermitage with frequent late afternoon service back to Rieti; it is better to purchase your ticket at a bar, or the Rieti train station, before boarding the train.

- Note that today's Camino is not part of the "Camino di Francesco" from Umbria to Rome you have been walking; though the yellow/blue signage is similar, this portion is part of the Rieti Camino of St. Francis.
- Continue to be vigilant around sheep dogs and guard dogs.

The Route:

Before you begin today's walk, a little background may be helpful. Civic leaders of the municipality of Rieti, in addition to the Lazio Province of OFM Franciscan friars, created a local walking Camino which connected the four Franciscan hermitages. This took place before the region of Umbria created the St. Francis Camino you have been walking along. Originally using wooden signposts, the Rieti Valley now uses yellow/blue signs similar to the ones you have been following. The main difference, however, is that the Rieti signage has the name of the hermitage on each one, with a directional arrow and distance to it.

Begin at the Roman bridge crossing the Velino River in the center of the city of Rieti. Standing on the modern bridge, look at the river on your left (upstream) and you will note the ancient Roman bridge now submerged mostly underwater. After crossing the river, turn right and walk along the jogging trail flanking the river alternating between charming parks and less scenic industrial areas. Follow the yellow/blue signs (marked with Fonte Colombo, and then Greccio) which will lead you on a stretch of about one kilometer next to a very busy road (more so in the morning during rush hour when you're likely to be here) with not much of a shoulder until you arrive at the outskirts of town.

A few kilometers from town, you will come to a pizza restaurant. Follow the signs into the woods on your left and you will soon begin a steep uphill climb on switchbacks. At the top of the hill, you will arrive at the Sanctuary of Fonte Colombo.

I recommend taking some time exploring the sanctuary complex including the church (pictured here) as well as the cave of Sacro Speco. Follow the signs down the paved path and you will pass a lovely chapel on your way to the cave where Francis prayed for forty days before he wrote his second Rule which was approved by Pope Honorius in 1223.

Next, walk across the parking lot and join the paved road uphill. Circle the village of Sant'Elia and pass the church of St. Elias the Prophet on your right. Then veer to the left and start slightly downhill. From here, the Camino saunters along beautiful and solitary country roads boasting scenic views of the Rieti Valley on your right, and the hills and mountains on your left.

After briefly re-joining the state highway, you will make your way through the tiny village of Piani Poggio Fidoni. Next, you will pass a short stretch along Via Tancia where you enter Val Canera. Leave the provincial road, and after a short jaunt uphill you will be in Colle Posta where there are more views in all directions. Behind you, to the south, is the Val Canera; to the northeast is the "Sacred Valley" of Rieti with Mount Terminillo towering to the east; not far in front of you to the north is the characteristic village of Contigliano and beyond it, in the distance ahead of you, you will begin to see your destination for the day: Greccio.

From here the Camino requires numerous short climbs and descents along more country roads shaded by Roverella trees. Soon you will come to the characteristic medieval town of Contigliano. After crossing through the village (a good place to stop for snacks or lunch), continue towards the town of Piano, taking the Onnina trail slightly uphill (this name is taken from the spring that flows into the locality of Piano di Contigliano). From here, you will walk towards the Abbey of San Pastore, which you might consider visiting if you have the time.

After passing the abbey on your left, follow the Camino which crosses the provincial road a few more times on the way to Greccio. After about thirty minutes, you will arrive in the town of Greccio. If you're there in time for lunch, you can enjoy a scrumptious meal at Nido del Corvo, as well as a striking view of the valley spread out below you and the towns of Poggio Bustone and Cantalice directly on the other side of the valley. Then continue along the paved road for your final two kilometers to the sanctuary of Greccio.

Referred to locally as the "New Bethlehem," Greccio is famed throughout the world as the site of the first nativity scene. Francis was frequently meditating on the life of Christ, including the incarnation; therefore, for Christmas of 1223, he desired to re-create an actual nativity scene with live animals to experience the feast in a new way.

Thomas of Celano wrote about the event:

> His highest aim, foremost desire, and greatest intention was to pay heed to the holy gospel in all things and through all things, to follow the teaching of our Lord Jesus Christ and to retrace His footsteps completely with all vigilance and all zeal, all the desire of his soul and all the fervor of his heart.

> Francis used to recall with regular meditation the words of Christ and recollect His deeds with most attentive perception. Indeed, so thoroughly did the humility of the Incarnation and the charity of the Passion occupy his memory that he scarcely wanted to think of anything else.

> We should note then, as matter worthy of memory and something to be recalled with reverence, what he did, three years prior to his death, at the town of Greccio, on the birthday of our Lord Jesus Christ. There was a certain man in that area named John who had a good reputation but an even better manner of life. Blessed Francis loved him with special affection, since, despite being a noble in the land and very honored in human society, he had trampled the

nobility of the flesh under his feet and pursued instead the nobility
of the spirit. As usual, blessed Francis had John summoned to him
some fifteen days prior to the birthday of the Lord. "If you desire
to celebrate the coming feast of the Lord together at Greccio," he
said to him, "hurry before me and carefully make ready the things
I tell you. For I wish to enact the memory of that babe who was
born in Bethlehem: to see as much as is possible with my own
bodily eyes the discomfort of his infant needs, how he lay in a
manger, and how, with an ox and an ass standing by, he rested on
hay." Once the good and faithful man had heard Francis's words,
he ran quickly and prepared in that place all the things that the holy
man had requested.

Finally, the day of joy has drawn near, the time of exultation has
come. From many different places the brethren have been called.
As they could, the men and women of that land with exultant hearts
prepare candles and torches to light up that night whose shining
star has enlightened every day and year. Finally, the holy man of
God comes and, finding all things prepared, he saw them and was
glad. Indeed, the manger is prepared, the hay is carried in, and the
ox and the ass are led to the spot. There simplicity is given a place
of honor, poverty is exalted, humility is commended, and out of
Greccio is made a new Bethlehem.

The night is lit up like day, delighting both man and beast. The
people arrive, ecstatic at this new mystery of new joy. The forest
amplifies the cries and the boulders echo back the joyful crowd.
The brothers sing, giving God due praise, and the whole night
abounds with jubilation. The holy man of God stands before the
manger, filled with heartfelt sighs, contrite in his piety, and
overcome with wondrous joy. Over the manger the solemnities of
the Mass are celebrated, and the priest enjoys a new consolation.

The holy man of God is dressed in the vestments of the Levites, since he was a Levite [i.e. deacon], and with full voice sings the holy gospel. Here is his voice: a powerful voice, a pleasant voice, a clear voice, a musical voice, inviting all to the highest of gifts. Then he preaches to the people standing around him and pours forth sweet honey about the birth of the poor King and the poor city of Bethlehem. Moreover, burning with excessive love, he often calls Christ the "babe from Bethlehem" whenever he means to call Him Jesus. Saying the word "Bethlehem" in the manner of a bleating sheep, he fills his whole mouth with sound but even more with sweet affection. He seems to lick his lips whenever he uses the expressions "Jesus" or "babe from Bethlehem," tasting the word on his happy palate and savoring the sweetness of the word. The gifts of the Almighty are multiplied there, and a virtuous man sees a wondrous vision. For the man saw a little child lying lifeless in the manger and he saw the holy man of God approach the child and waken him from a deep sleep. Nor is this vision unfitting, since in the hearts of many the child Jesus has been given over to oblivion. Now he is awakened and impressed on their loving memory by His own grace through His holy servant Francis. At length, the night's solemnities draw to a close and everyone went home with joy.

The hay placed in the manger there was preserved afterwards so that, through it, the Lord might restore to health the pack animals and the other animals there, as He multiplied his holy mercy. It came to pass in the surrounding area that many of the animals, suffering from various diseases, were freed from their illnesses when they ate some of this hay. What is more, women who had been suffering with long and hard labor had an easy delivery after they placed some of this hay upon themselves. Finally, an entire group of people of both sexes obtained much-desired relief from an assortment of afflictions.

At last, the site of the manger was consecrated as a temple of the Lord. In honor of the most blessed father Francis, an altar was constructed over the manger, and a church was dedicated. This was done so that where animals once ate the fodder of the hay, there humans henceforth for healing of body and soul would eat the flesh of the immaculate and spotless lamb, our Lord Jesus Christ, who gave Himself for us with supreme and indescribable love, who lives and rules with the Father and the Holy Spirit as God, eternally glorious forever and ever. Amen. Alleluia, Alleluia.

(Thomas of Celano, *First Life*, Chapter 30, 466-71)

From Greccio you can return to Rieti by train, but the station is another four kilometers (downhill, though). Descend the staircase from the hermitage down to the coffee bar. Turn left and walk along the windy Via dei Frati paved road to the valley floor. At the gas station on the main provincial road, go left toward Sellecchia, then in about 500 meters, go right on Via Montisola and then make a quick right again to the quiet train station. Trains pass every hour or so and in eighteen minutes, after stopping only in Contigliano, you'll be back in the center of Rieti – a testament to the marvels of modern transportation. Note that tickets (for just €1.50) should be purchased at a Tabacchi shop prior to boarding, though you may be able to buy one from the conductor on board.

Franciscan places on the route:

- The Sanctuary of Fonte Colombo is a delightful hermitage perched on a hill in the thick of nature. Its original Latin name, *Fons Colombarum*, derives from a group of doves (*colombae*) who were known to drink from a spring here (*fons*).
- Visit the simple church, the chapel dedicated to Mary Magdalene, the Chapel of St. Michael, and the Sacro Speco grotto. It was in this

cave where Saint Francis prayed and fasted for forty days between 1222 and 1223 before writing his final Rule. Known as the *Regula Bullata*, or Stamped Bull, it was approved in 1223 by Pope Honorius. Additionally, somewhere in this complex Francis underwent a painful operation on his eyes sometime around 1225 or 1226. The word crèche comes from the name of this town, adapted into English through the French.

- In Greccio, make sure you visit the cave where the Mass took place, the early thirteenth-century hermitage (including the cell where Francis slept), the fourteenth-century dormitory (including the cell where St. Bernardine of Siena slept), and the choir and church. Inside the modern church is an exhibit of different nativity scenes in the tradition of the school of Naples, as well as nativity scenes from elsewhere in Italy and Europe.

Other places of interest:

- Abbey of San Pastore

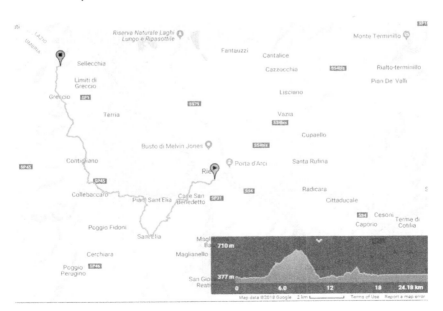

Rieti to Rome

The St. Francis Camino can be broken down into two sections: Assisi to Rieti and Rieti to Rome. Rieti is not only the center of Italy geographically (there is a square and monument in Rieti marking the mathematical center of Italy), it is just beyond the halfway point of the Camino between Assisi and Rome.

From Rieti southward, there are fewer "memories" of St. Francis until you get to Rome. Though the more rugged Apennine terrain is mostly behind you, the rolling terrain of the hilly Sabine region and the Via Salaria — plus longer daily stages – still make for some tough walking. Given this, many pilgrims — especially those looking for a more "Franciscan" experience — prefer to finish their Camino in Rieti or Greccio.

However, for those pilgrims who wish for more, the route south of Rieti boasts plenty to make it worthwhile: protected nature preserves, archaeological sites, medieval ruins, and the Eternal City itself.

Most importantly, however, for the pilgrim walking in the footsteps of St. Francis, is the truly awesome arrival at one of the most visited pilgrimage sites in the world: St. Peter's Basilica. In this, you are truly walking in the footsteps of St. Francis — as well as countless pilgrims who have gone before.

Stage 10: From Rieti to Poggio San Lorenzo
Distance: 22 kilometers
Cumulative increase in altitude: + 499 m
Cumulative loss of altitude: - 377 m
Surface: asphalt roads, gravel roads, dirt trails, country roads
Time: 7 hours
Difficulty: Moderate
Relive Video: relive.cc/view/vXOnEyk1dBv

A trek along the modern and ancient Via Salaria, through woods, over streams and fields of Lazio's ancient Sabina region dotted with vestiges of Roman history.

Daily Franciscan Spirituality/reflection: Peace

- Francis wrote: "The Lord revealed to me a greeting, as we used to say: "May the Lord give you peace." (*Testament* 23)
- The phrase, *Pax et Bonum* (Peace and goodness), is a well-known Franciscan maxim.
- Despite the severe forms of conflict and violence in the High Middle Ages, Francis found peace in his Christian life: through poverty by renouncing his worldly possessions and inheritance, through the

penances he embraced, through humility and nonviolence, through the community in which he lived, through his service to others especially the poorest, and through the Church he was part of.

- Peace comes through embracing nonviolence, forgiveness and charity practiced toward others.
- Is there anyone you have not forgiven? Or people to whom you do not practice charity?
- What are some areas within your own life, family, parish, or community where there is a lack of peace? Can you think of a way to bring peace to that situation?

Route notes:

- Unfortunately, the frequency, upkeep, and reliability of yellow/blue signposts are spotty once you get south of Rieti. You risk getting lost without GPX tracks or a good guidebook or map.
- Continue to be vigilant for dogs.

The Route:

From upper Rieti, walk down Via Roma and cross the bridge over the Velino River. Though some guidebooks, and the GPX tracks, have you turn left just after the bridge, stay straight on Via Roma so you can visit Rieti's famed Porta Romana (ancient Roman city gate). Once the gateway from Rieti to Rome on the Via Salaria, you will be either on or near this storied road for much of the rest of the way to Rome.

At the Roman gate, turn left and begin heading out of town. Cross under the highway and look to your left where there is a large nativity scene dedicated to peace on the side of the hill.

Continue a short distance and you'll come to an important water bottling facility on the ancient springs of Cottorella. These springs have made Rieti famous; and today, thanks to modern aqueducts, supply a large amount of drinking water for Rome's three million inhabitants. There is a fountain here if you wish to fill up with Rieti's famed water which locals say has a healthy high alkaline PH.

At the water facility, note a milestone: a signpost pointing left and indicating just "100 km a Roma". Almost there!

Stay on the paved road and in a few minutes keep your head up for a yellow/blue sign on your right leading you off the road, over a stream on a wooden bridge, and through a field to the modern Via Salaria.

Once you reach the Via Salaria — framed by rows of tall trees — walk along the left shoulder of the busy Salaria until you are able to scramble down to a foot path a more comfortable distance from the busy road. This is the modern Via Salaria built by Mussolini in the 1920s, though it is not necessarily overlaying the famed ancient Via Salaria.

Stay on the Camino for about three kilometers along or near the Via Salaria with the Ariana and Turano streams to your left until you come to the town of Maglianello Basso. Continue walking in the valley along the banks of the Ariana until you come to the town of San Giovanni Reatino on your right with a Go Kart track on your left. Follow the yellow/blue sign to the left here and you will peel away from the Via Salaria. Now you'll follow a dirt trail flanking the "fosso Ariana." (Note that some recent reports are that the trail suffered serious erosion due to heavy rains; do your best to walk safely around the compromised ground.)

Continue along the dirt road which leads to a paved road. Though there is little traffic out here in the country, stay to the side of the road as Italian motorists are not used to pedestrians walking in the road. Just when you start to wonder if you're in the right place, you'll see an encouraging yellow/blue sign indicating to turn off the asphalt road onto a dirt trail to the right. Follow the Camino downhill then back uphill until you reach the ancient Roman bridge, Sambuco.

After poking around the bridge, get ready for a serious uphill climb. When you reach the paved road at the top of the hill, take a few minutes to catch your breath and appreciate the beautiful panorama all around you.

Here you might consider taking a detour to your right where you can make a pitstop in the sleepy town of Ornaro Basso for some vittles at its sit-down restaurant (which may or may not be open) or a grocery store which is open every day and whose shop owner will prepare you an inexpensive sandwich with local products.

Leave Ornaro Basso and backtrack to the Camino to where you left the trail. Soon you'll pass another reminder of Rome's omnipresent past — an ancient Roman mile marker on the Via Salaria from the era of Caesar Augustus — today nonchalantly integrated in the garden of a local homeowner.

Follow the road downhill on a somewhat paved road. At the bottom, the asphalt ends as you prepare for your last steep, though short, climb of the day.

At the top of the hill you'll come to a paved road. Note that the yellow/blue sign points left toward the city of Torricella in Sabina. However, if your destination is in Poggio San Lorenzo (at the Agritourism Santa Giusta, for example), go right. In either case, make sure you spend a little time in Poggio San Lorenzo, as it is a charming historical town.

Other places of interest:

- Fonte Cottorella: the Cottorella thermal springs have been used since ancient times, and the Romans themselves often had recourse to natural springs and thermal baths not just for relaxation, but for health. Modern science, in fact, has confirmed that high PH water (alkaline) can improve health both through consumption and bathing in thermal baths.

- Ponte Sambuco: the bridge Ponte Sambuco is an extraordinarily well-preserved ancient Roman bridge constructed as part of the Via Salaria road to cross the Ariana creek; originally built in the fourth century BC, the actual bridge is from the first century AD.

- Poggio San Lorenzo: though you may be overnighting at the welcoming San Giusta agritourism, make sure you visit the town of Poggio San Lorenzo. Though today just 500 inhabitants, it boasts a stately past as an important hill town and stopover point along the Via Salaria; visit the church of San Lorenzo, patron and namesake of the city.

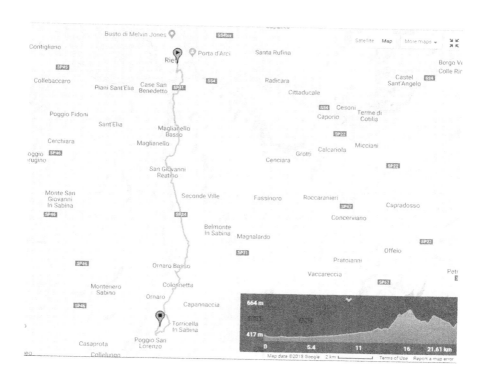

Stage 11: From Poggio San Lorenzo to Ponticelli
Distance: 23 kilometers
Cumulative increase in altitude: + 821 m
Cumulative loss of altitude: - 1015 m
Surface: asphalt road, gravel roads
Time: 8 hours
Difficulty: Very Difficult
Relive Video: relive.cc/view/vPv4JPdXm36

Today involves some tough climbs rewarded by gorgeous views of nature along with a smattering of Roman ruins and ancient churches. Don't miss the church of Santa Vittoria, one of the highlights of today's stage.

Daily Franciscan Spirituality/reflection: Peacemaker

- Francis wrote: "The true peacemakers are those who preserve peace of mind and body for love of our Lord Jesus Christ, despite what they suffer in this world." (Admonitions 15).
- Francis is known as a peacemaker to others. He often sought to reconcile civil wars in various towns and cities, or feuds between noble families or between civil leaders and clerics.

- Francis arrived in towns in a simple manner dressed in poverty. People could see peace within him, and they listened. He had renounced everything – money, position, politics, and worldly honors. As he had dispossessed himself of everything, he approached conflicts from the outside and people did not feel threatened by him. As he traveled around preaching, his example was much more convincing than the words he preached.
- What was it about Francis that led him to being a peacemaker?
- Do you consider yourself a peacemaker? Reflect on a time in which you brought peace to a difficult situation.

Route notes:

- Today's stage involving four climbs into towns, if not for its distance, make for a challenging day.
- Today's stage is notorious for barking dogs — particularly after Poggio Moiano.

The Route:

If you haven't yet visited the town of Poggio San Lorenzo, the Camino passes through it on your way out in just under two kilometers from Santa Giusta. Its quaint city center and Roman walls are worthy of a visit.

After leaving Poggio San Lorenzo, follow the switchback to the valley floor. In front of you is the first climb of the day; from the other side you have a wonderful view looking back at Poggio San Lorenzo.

Follow the Camino through the woods and hills, and into a grove of olive trees. Go downhill to the road leading to the town of Monteleone Sabino where you have the option of heading into town or not. (There is not much to see there, but there are stores and coffee bars.)

Once back on the Camino, you will come across a fascinating archaeological site known as Trebula Mutuesca, which boasts the ruins of an ancient Roman theater, baths, and pavement with mosaics. There is a fine archeological museum here, for a fee, if you have the time and interest (and it's open).

Just past the archaeological area, follow the Camino through a large field to an old farmhouse on the far side. Then walk toward the fantastic Romanesque church dedicated to Santa Vittoria, an early Roman martyr saint. Though it is often closed, perhaps you will be graced with an open door in which case you will be able to view the catacombs and a well, known for its legendary healing water.

Now follow the asphalt road past the memorial for fallen soldiers, then through orchards and olive groves until you turn left into the woods.

The trail ends at a local road where you will eventually pass the church of San Martino upon entering the village of Poggio Moiano perched on a hill.

In Poggio Moiano, you can stop and rest and admire the lovely Palazzo Baronale and the church of San Giovanni Battista.

Leaving Poggio Moiano, follow the Camino down to the valley floor, over an ancient stone bridge, then up another steep hill. Get ready for some barking dogs (hopefully the infamous penned male Rottweiler is calm today). Now walk over the plains and then along the base of Monte Calvo to your right. You'll soon begin a descent on an asphalt road into the town of Ponticelli with the cemetery on your right.

Accommodations are somewhat limited in Ponticelli; if you want to splurge, there is the renovated posh Orsini castle in the nearby town of Nerola (the castle you see in the distance to the southwest).

If you have time and energy still, you may wish to visit the lovely Franciscan sanctuary of Santa Maria delle Grazie, though it is almost three kilometers from town and on the other side of the valley.

Other places of interest:

- Monteleone Sabino
- Archeological Area of Trebula Mutuesca
- Church of Santa Vittoria
- Poggio Moiano

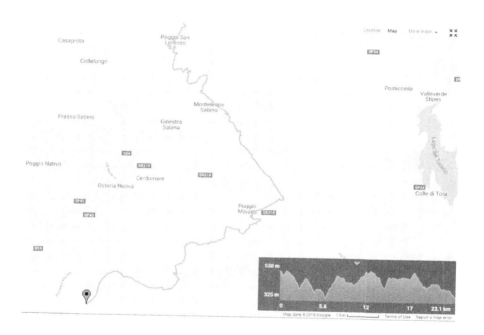

Stage 12: From Ponticelli to Monterotondo
Distance: 30 kilometers
Cumulative increase in altitude: + 690 m
Cumulative loss of altitude: - 871 m
Surface: paths, asphalt road, dirt roads
Time: 9 hours
Difficulty: Very Difficult
Relive Video: relive.cc/view/vWqBe2ZM9Y6

From the hilly region of Sabina to the open Tiber River valley, today's long stage is rich in nature and farmland. It continues through more undulating olive groves and orchards through the natural reserve of Macchia di Gattaceca to Monterotondo.

Daily Franciscan Spirituality/reflection: Evangelization

- Francis wrote: "All the brothers, however, should preach by their deeds." (The Rule of 1221, Chap 17, 3).
- Thomas of Celano quotes Francis as saying, "The preacher must first draw from secret prayers what he will later pour out in holy sermons; he must first grow hot within before he speaks words that are in themselves cold."

- Francis' attitude toward evangelization was that before announcing Christ, we should imitate Christ; before proclaiming the Gospel, we had to live the Gospel; before exhorting others to do penance, we should be a penitent; before preaching about peace, we should have peace in our own hearts.
- It is believed that St. Francis never intended to start a community or have people follow him; he desired simply to follow Jesus and the Gospel. Yet in doing so, his way of life was attractive to others and many men and women began following him.
- Who influenced your spiritual life the most? Was it your parents, someone else, or both? What was it about them that influenced you? Take a minute to write about the things they did or said that influenced you.
- How do you think your Christian life influences others? Has anyone ever told you that you have made a difference in their life? How?

Route notes:

- Today's stage is difficult mostly due to the distance, but also because of the hills.
- Some participants prefer to split today's stage in half and overnight in Montelibretti, the halfway point.

The Route:

Begin your day surrounded by olive groves and oak trees on paved and dirt roads. Once you pass the town of Poggio Corese on your left, note the Orsini castle in the town of Nerola beyond on your left. Continue toward the town of Acquaviva (eight kilometers from starting point), where you may wish to stop and take a break.

Continue another five kilometers among a landscape, still in the Sabine region, punctuated by olive groves, large orchards and cultivated fields. Go down into the valley and then up again to the town of Montelibretti, home to the charming Barberini Palace. An inviting place to take a break is a tasty pastry shop and bar just after you come into town.

After leaving Montelibretti, you'll walk for a stretch along the Via Nomentana, another ancient consular road built by the Romans from Rome some twenty-three kilometers to modern Mentana.

As you continue walking, in the distance you will begin to see the thirteenth-century Torre della Fiora (Fiora Tower), which almost seems to follow and watch over you as you continue through the countryside of Lazio.

After the tower, enjoy the gentle Macchia di Gattaceca nature reserve with its smoother landscape — dotted by fields of wheat and pastures — until Monterotondo comes into view.

Just before arriving in Monterotondo, you have to negotiate your way underneath a busy highway. Pay attention here as it is sometimes difficult to stay on the Camino underneath the highway; trust your GPX tracks, as well as the yellow arrows painted on the ground (added after feedback from not a few hapless pilgrims!).

After walking a while on the sometimes-overgrown path, you will arrive at a traffic signal in the outskirts of Monterotondo. Here you can either follow the yellow/blue signs that will take you to the left around town along the Via Nomentana (this passes by a McDonald's in the event you're nostalgic for some non-Italian fare), or else you can go straight at the traffic signal and enter town that way.

Monterotondo is a quaint town with plenty of café bars and eateries, a *corso* (promenade) for evening strolls, good pizzerias, and even a movie theater. Once fought over for its strategic defensive position along the Via Salaria by storied Roman families like Barberini and Orsini, today Monterotondo is a lively Roman commuter suburb.

Other places of interest:

- Torre della Fiora
- Natural Reserve Macchia di Gattaceca
- Monterotondo

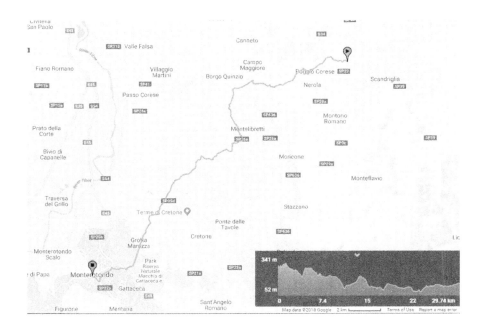

Stage 13: From Monterotondo to Monte Sacro
Distance: 19 kilometers
Cumulative increase in altitude: + 311 m
Cumulative loss of altitude: - 422 m
Surface: asphalt road, gravel roads
Time: 6 hours
Difficulty: Moderate
Relive Video: relive.cc/view/vRO7d49rnK6

From Roman countryside to urban landscape of the Eternal City: St. Peter's is close.

Daily Franciscan Spirituality/reflection: Mary

- By now, you have come across countless *"edicole"*, or wayside devotional shrines dedicated to the saints, especially the Virgin Mary.
- In Catholic and Franciscan spirituality, Mary is not just simply the mother of Jesus, or just one of the early committed disciples, but she is the Mother of the Mystical Body of Christ.
- Devotion to Mary was a foundational part of Francis's spiritual life, and she was the perfect model to imitate.

Then, suddenly, you're evicted from the peaceful reserve onto a loud road, Via della Marcigliana, a short jaunt from Cinquina, the beginning of anti-aesthetic urban Roman sprawl which will accompany you for the rest of your journey to St. Peter's. On a positive note, the benefits of walking in an urban milieu are that you can stop whenever you like to purchase a beverage, eat, and have access to real toilets.

Next, follow the busy road, Via Bufalotta, pretty much the rest of the way to Monte Sacro.

When you arrive in Monte Sacro, you may wish to visit the church of Santi Angeli Custodi (Holy Guardian Angels) for some respite from the chaotic nature of the city; they also have a nice pilgrim's stamp in the sacristy.

Other places of interest:

- Natural Reserve of Marcigliana
- Archaeological remains of Crustumerium
- Church of Santi Angeli Custodi in Monte Sacro

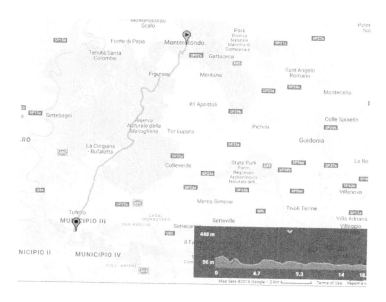

189

Stage 14: From Monte Sacro to St. Peter's
Distance: 16 kilometers
Cumulative increase in altitude: + 158 m
Cumulative loss of altitude: - 168 m
Surface: urban sidewalks, bike paths
Time: 5 hours
Difficulty: Easy
Relive Video: relive.cc/view/vRO7d49kry6

*A rewarding easy walk along riverside bike paths and sidewalks
to your final destination: St. Peter's Basilica.*

Daily Franciscan Spirituality/reflection: Catholic Church

- Though some today claim "spirituality not religion," Francis of Assisi, in this, was no model.
- Referred to in his day as a staunch *"Vir Catholicus"* (Catholic Man), Francis willfully strove to ensure that his religious Order would be and remain within the canonical context of the Catholic Church: he sought approval to live his way of life from Pope Innocent III in 1209; he followed the counsel and direction of Bishops and Popes;

he allowed Church teachings, councils, and directives to guide him; and all the while, he was edified by the sacraments (especially the Eucharist), Scripture, and devotion to the saints (especially Mary).

- Yet, Francis's relationship to the Church remained unique, and despite his faith in the Church, he never sought to become a priest, canon, or monk – the common religious vocations of his era. Instead, he struggled to create a unique spiritual movement within the official canonical structure of the Catholic Church. In fact, through his novel movement, he renewed the Church, rather than rejecting it and separating from it.

- A story is recounted by Stephen of Bourbon, a 13th century Dominican, of how Francis, on a preaching tour through the villages, was told of a cleric who was living with a concubine. Instead of rejecting or criticizing the priest, Francis went to the priest, prostrated himself, kissed his hands, and said, "I do not really know whether these hands are stained as the other man claims they are. In any case, I do know that, even if they are, this in no way lessens the power and efficacy of the sacraments of God; those hands remain the channel whereby God's graces and blessings stream down on the people."

- Do you belong to a church? If so, what is your relationship with your church like?

- If you have been hurt by someone in the church, can you still find the greater blessings of belonging to a church, instead of separating from it?

Route notes:

- Though in the heart of urban Rome, the Camino has been designed to avoid the busiest streets and takes you on riverside bike paths through some parks.

- To get your Testimonium, you can go to either the sacristy within St. Peter's basilica, or the ORP office in the Pio XII square.

The Route:

From the main church of Angeli Custodi in Monte Sacro, cross the bridge over the Aniene River. Go right and follow the Camino along sidewalks and jogging paths.

When you arrive at Villa Ada, the Camino does not enter the park; instead it has you skirt the park (which will be on the other side of a wall on your left) as you walk along a busy street. However, this is Rome's second largest park and may be worth a visit: Villa Ada was originally built as a royal residence for the reigning Savoy family and the park is known for its architecture and greenery.

Pass the mosque, and then another park (Villa Glori), then a concert hall on your left. After you go underneath an overpass, you will arrive at the road, Viale Tiziano (which parallels Via Flaminia). Here, the "official" Camino route has you turn right and in less than one kilometer you'll be at the famed Milvian Bridge. Here, in the year 312 AD, Emperor Constantine defeated Maxentius after seeing a vision of a cross in the sky, the *Chi Rho*, and the words, "*In hoc signo vinces*" ("In this sign, you will conquer"). He had his troops wear the same cross on their armor and he was victorious. He soon ended the persecutions against Christianity by legalizing Christianity (in the Edict of Milan) paving the way for Christianity to become the official religion of the Roman Empire.

From Ponte Milvio, the official Camino route crosses the bridge and flanks the west side of the Tiber River all the way to St. Peter's.

However, a more interesting and historic route would be to backtrack from Ponte Milvio, walking south along the Via Flaminia, into the historic center of Rome at Piazza del Popolo. In fact, this was the ancient entranceway for pilgrims into the city, as the Villa Borghese gardens, adjacent to Piazza del Popolo, were intended to welcome pilgrims coming into the Eternal city. The Via Flaminia was the ancient Roman road that traversed the peninsula all the way to the Adriatic Sea (passing through Foligno near Assisi).

If you choose the ancient route (off the trail and GPX tracks), walk south from Ponte Milvio along sidewalks until you arrive at the ancient city gate in front of you. To the left are the Borghese gardens while through the gate is Rome's Piazza del Popolo, a delightful and major tourist spot in Rome. Immediately to your left inside the gate is the church of Santa Maria del Popolo boasting two famous paintings by Caravaggio, Baroque master of chiaroscuro: "Conversion of Saint Paul" and "Crucifixion of Saint Peter." Piazza del Popolo is a nice place to rest or snack before you make your final journey into St. Peter's.

From the middle of the square, there are three roads in front of you. Take the one to the right and continue straight. Along the way you will have your first glimpses of the Tiber River on your right, and you will pass the recently excavated mausoleum of Caesar Augustus and the famed *Ara Pacis* museum housing the ancient "Altar of Peace" constructed to honor Caesar Augustus's victorious military campaigns.

Turn right at Via Sant'Agostino and in a few meters, you will arrive at the northern entrance to Piazza Navona which will be on your left. Piazza Navona was originally a stadium built by Emperor Domitian for chariot races and "games" in the first century AD but is now one of Rome's main attractions famed for Baroque era fountains and churches. If you choose not to visit the square now, at least peer down to your left where you can see the ancient archway that once served as the entrance to the Domitian stadium.

Continue straight and enter the somewhat non-descript road, Via dei Coronari. This quaint street takes its name from the rosary-makers who lined the street centuries ago crafting and selling "crown rosaries" and other religious souvenirs to the hordes of pilgrims traipsing to and from St. Peter's (arriving likely in the same condition you are right now). You won't find any vendors selling religious articles these days, as Via dei Coronari is today lined with tony boutiques and high-end art galleries.

Follow Via dei Coronari until it dead ends. Now get ready for a dramatic welcome to your destination: turn right and allow the angels of the striking "Holy Angels" bridge and castle to greet and accompany you to St. Peter's. Cross the bridge, walk by Castel Sant'Angelo (originally a mausoleum for Emperor Hadrian, later a fortress to watch over the Tiber River and protect the pope), and walk along Via della Conciliazione into St. Peter's.

Despite the hordes of tourists and pilgrims all around you, this last stretch is a good time to remain in silence and reflect on what you have just accomplished. As you approach the place where St. Peter was martyred and buried, think about your journey: what you have been through and accomplished to get here.

It should be said that pilgrims sometimes feel a letdown when they arrive in St. Peter's. Unfortunately, you must endure the rigmarole of entering the basilica, including security and long waits together with the hordes of tourists and "bus pilgrims." And you may experience the brusqueness Romans are sometimes known for as they confiscate your pocketknives and walking poles which are necessary for the Camino but forbidden in the basilica, and nonchalantly gab with one another indifferent to the elation you are probably feeling now. (Note which metal detector you went through so that you can retrieve any confiscated items after you leave the basilica.)

If you have a few more days in Rome, there are plenty of guidebooks and websites that describe in detail the Eternal City as well as the Vatican. If you have a limited amount of time, I recommend any of the hop-on hop-off tour buses. ORP (Opera Romana Pellegrinaggi) operates one with an emphasis on the Christian sites of Rome.

If you wish to continue your Franciscan experience, make sure you visit the church of San Francesco a Ripa in the Trastevere district: it was this area where St. Francis stayed when he came to Rome as there was a leper hospital nearby. Don't miss the copy of an alleged portrait of St. Francis, in addition to the cell where the saint lived and a black stone he used as a pillow.

Franciscan places near the route:

- San Francesco in Ripa

Other places on the route:

- Vatican City
- Ponte Milvio (Milvian Bridge)
- Piazza del Popolo (People's Square)
- Piazza Navona (Navona Square)
- Castel Sant'Angelo (Holy Angel Castle)

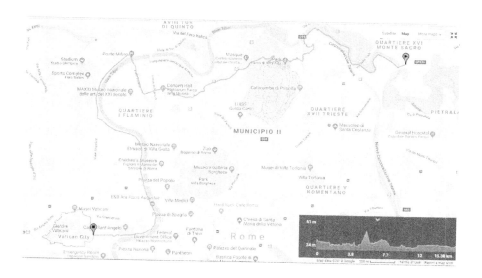

AT THE CONCLUSION OF
THE JOURNEY

Receiving your Testimonium *is a special moment and is a well-deserved reward. Here, in fact, just before or after receiving it, I recommend entering the Eucharistic Adoration chapel (halfway down St. Peter's nave on the right) where you can spend some moments giving thanks to God for having brought you here successfully, and safely.*

Take some time to reflect on the following reflections and questions.

In the story of the Transfiguration on Mount Tabor, the disciples wished to remain with Christ in his glory a little bit longer. Peter said, "Lord, it is good that we are here. If you wish, I will make three tents here...," Mt. 17:4. Instead, Jesus led them back down the mountain.

The same can apply to your pilgrimage. While it may be nice to remain in the space, the time eventually comes to leave and return home. Here are some prayers for the journey down the mountain of your local pilgrimage experience.

As you leave this sanctuary, the goal to your pilgrimage, consider the journey that is now in front of you and beginning. Perhaps the Lord has revealed the next stage of your life or given you great clarification, or perhaps he is asking you to continue to listen and pray.

Whatever this pilgrimage leads you toward, continue to ask for God's guidance and protection, and be open to your next pilgrimage destination, in the world or in your heart.

Pray an *Our Father*, *Hail Mary*, and *Glory Be*, and ask the intercession of Sts. Peter, James, and John to accompany you as you "make your way down the mountain."

Take some time to reflect on the following questions:

- Was there any event, person, place, or experience on the pilgrimage that was particularly impressing? Why?
- Where have you experienced transformation on this pilgrimage?
- Do you have any new insights after this pilgrimage?
- Has this pilgrimage changed the way you see things?
- Do you see God differently?
- What does spirituality mean to you now?
- Do you see the sacredness in your own life story? In the simplicity, the 'ordinariness'? Do you see God's love and grace in it?
- What has your life journey been like? Do you see your own life as a pilgrimage?
- How can you continue to grow in holiness?
- What do the lives of the saints have in common? How can you imitate them?
- Are you challenged to change your spiritual life in any way?
- Where do you see God's impressions, graces, the Holy Spirit in the world? In people, places, history?
- What was the culture like in which you grew up? How has this new culture changed the way you see your homeland?
- What are the strengths of your culture?
- Where do you experience God's grace in your culture?
- What are some faults of your culture? How can you guard yourself against falling into them? Can you do anything to change them?
- Are you grateful for your country, heritage, background? Do you recognize the complexity of cultures – that there is good and bad in all people?
- In what ways is the Church strong where you live? How can it improve?
- How did you experience Church on this pilgrimage?
- Has this pilgrimage led you to do anything differently when you return home?

OBTAINING YOUR *TESTIMONIUM*

There are two places from which you can receive your final stamp in your *Credenziale* Passport and pick up your *Testimonium*. The most memorable, in my opinion, is from the sacristy within St. Peter's basilica; The sacristy is through the doorway on the left side of the nave just before the transept. The sacristy may be a more memorable experience; however, it closes during midday, likely the time in which you will be arriving. If you'll be in Rome for a few days, you may opt to come back the following day or wait until it re-opens in the afternoon.

Otherwise, you can receive your stamp and *Testimonium* at the Opera Romana Pellegrinaggi (ORP) Vatican pilgrimage office in Pio XII square on the south side of the piazza between St. Peter's Square and Via della Conciliazione. The certificate here is identical, but the stamp is different from the one in St. Peter's.

Just a reminder: to receive the "testimonium" certificate, you need to have walked a minimum of 100 kilometers along the Camino, and they do not have to be contiguous. Regardless, the testimonium is almost always issued without anyone actually questioning or calculating how far you actually walked.

EPILOGUE

PILGRIM'S EXPERIENCES ON THE ST. FRANCIS CAMINO

Following are how previous pilgrims have responded to the question:
"How would you describe walking the entire Way of Francis Camino as well as the fitness level required to complete it?"

"Make sure you are fit and ready for a strenuous walking experience. The walk includes some serious uphill jaunts, not to mention daily distances in the 20 km (12.5 mile) range; so, it's a very smart idea to start a training regime early if this level of physical exertion sounds daunting. Some walkers I've accompanied in the past confessed that their training did not meet their own expectations, and though they made it to the goal they took about 30% longer to walk the early stages than planned, which means less time to relax and recuperate each day. Be well-prepared against blisters and bring a blister kit. You'll want to prevent blisters by working out your combination of socks and shoes or boots in advance, as well as training on varied terrain over long distances. This is even more important than adequate cardio training, since the #1 reason people don't finish a pilgrimage walk is they develop painful blisters! Lastly, pack in a wise and thoughtful manner. Packing heavy suitcases and packs will make life difficult for you."

Sandy Brown, author of *The Way of Francis*

"Minimum preparation should be the ability to hike 14-16 miles with elevation changes. Better preparation would be to walk 40 miles per week, including a 14-16-mile hike with elevation changes. [...] One of the biggest insights that I've gained from this pilgrimage was the very strong sense and powerful nature of community that existed between [our group of six that departed together]. And how we really were only able to conquer many hardships — blisters, sore muscles, aching feet, fear of heights, hot weather, and terrain/physical challenges that some were not accustomed to — because of the power of our community. In our disparate little group, we brought many gifts that supplemented each other. In retrospect, we really were not prepared physically to hike [some difficult stretches] or the entire 101 miles, but we did. […]! All in all, it was a profound spiritual experience!"

Diane Gaidon, Long Island, NY, USA

"Please reference the physical aspect as well as anything else you consider important. Again, they need to understand that it can be strenuous. I believe sometimes any of us can over or underestimate our physical ability. I have had the privilege of being on a number of Franciscan pilgrimages over the years. They were all excellent; but this walking pilgrimage was different. Walking the route that St. Francis took to Rome somehow connected you even more to the history of this saint and his powerful presence in the church. The beauty surrounding you on this walk was in itself a very spiritual experience of God's presence."

Fr. Fred Wendel, Georgia, USA

"It is one thing to be able to talk and read about something but to be able to go and experience it just adds to your understanding and interaction with it. That was definitely the case here since we were able to go to the places St. Francis did and hear the stories about him while standing where he stood. There were times that were strenuous and other times that the trail was easy. The times that were tougher I found myself wondering how much harder it was for St. Francis or any other pilgrims to walk those paths that weren't marked with the signs to keep them on track. I gained an even greater appreciation for creation while on this pilgrimage, I love noticing small detailed things like a caterpillar on a leaf but also experiencing big things like standing on a high point of the mountain to see a great view. I feel that I can relate to St. Francis in the fact that he also paid attention to the small things like animals and bugs but also the "small" people who were outcasts during his time but he also looked at the bigger picture of how to be a servant to God."

Ashley Doran, Iowa, USA

"The Way of St. Francis Camino is a beautiful, spiritual, but physically challenging Camino. The opportunity to see the country [Francis] walked and feel his impact is unique, and to have his life and journeys explained was wonderful. The physical act of walking is a body mantra which enables one to move from thinking to being. In order for this to happen effectively, the walker need to be quite fit, not just for walking long distances consistently, but fit enough to manage hard climbs, uncertain and uneven terrain. The nature of the terrain is challenging, but to a large extent one becomes fit during the walk. The spirituality of this Camino is hard to name: for some it may encompass walking; for others, visiting the places St. Francis lived and ministered; for others still the silence and the beauty; or the company of other pilgrims. HOWEVER, one could not walk the journey without being affected within one's soul. Walking the first few days was wonderfully stilling and beautiful. Yet, in retrospect, my highlight was walking into the Vatican and seeing the Holy City, it was a bit overwhelming really. I wonder how St. Francis, and St. Benedict and other must have felt when they arrived at the same place."

Rev. Catie Inches-Ogden, Australia

"To do this walk you need an open heart to experience the pure joy of your faith. The pilgrimage will touch you in ways you never expected. You need to be in good physical shape and train. The trails will challenge you, but the walk is so much part of the journey. It gives you time, in the most beautiful surroundings and helps you to process life's challenges. It allows you time to talk with your fellow pilgrimage and learn from them. You also have the opportunity to walk alone and get to know yourself. A pilgrimage is something one should do for themselves on a regular basis. You are not the same person by the end of your journey!"

Karen Harmon, Ontario, Canada

"Unless you can train in similar terrain, this walk is extremely challenging and is more suitable for individuals that are experienced in trekking in areas with significant ascents and descents. I am 51 years of age, had physical limitations with my right knee, and had to use an expensive knee brace and walking sticks to complete my daily walks. Without the knee brace and the walking sticks, as well as the less strenuous options offered, I would not have been able to complete the pilgrimage successfully. In the end, I walked approximately 113 miles and feel blessed to have done so; but, yes, it was extremely challenging! And, one more thing, I wore very expensive hiking boots that I had "broken in" and trained with prior to the pilgrimage. I only ended up with one blister and the boots, while very costly, did also make a difference in me being able to complete the pilgrimage. Therefore, you need to make sure you have high quality gear for this pilgrimage; otherwise, your feet and body WILL suffer! Lastly, my husband, who is a retired Marine from the United States Marine Corps and served in the Infantry (therefore he did many extensive marches/walks throughout his military career carrying extremely heavy backpacks), said that this pilgrimage was very physically challenging! He also said that the expensive hiking boots I bought him made a significant difference – he ended up with NO blisters!"

Ruth Goldberg, Sigonella NATO Base, Sicily

"[This pilgrimage] is not the same as the pilgrimage to Santiago. The climbs [on the St. Francis Camino] are more difficult and the path not as well marked. There are fewer places to stay and stop along the way. One needs to be prepared to be flexible, be challenged physically, be patient with fellow pilgrims and be moved spiritually. Having said that, the walking pilgrimage has the potential to change your perspective on what is important in life... I had a great experience: it was challenging, rewarding, frustrating, liberating, spiritual, and emotional. I'm sure I'll be processing it for a while to come."

Michelle DeMers, Texas, USA

"It ain't easy. [...] Some of the walks, the steep climbs and the loose rocks, both in ascents and descents [are very difficult]. I would describe the soreness of the first four days, and then, the miracle of this body God designed when the soreness went away, and the body-machine started to work efficiently. I had not experienced that since high school football, and it was a nice revelation all over again. ... [Regarding training for hills] there is no way I could have simulated them near Charlotte on a regular basis. I walked 40+ miles each week in preparation but was unprepared for the steepness and length of the hills. That being said, we all made it. It was part of the sacrifice of the pilgrimage and I think a good beginning bonding experience for the participants. [My highlight was] walking in the flat, rural areas. The sunshine, the fruit on the trees and vines, the sheep, feeling my heartbeat and my legs work. Simply a sense of God everywhere. I expected good exercise, a closeness to nature, a spiritual retreat of sorts and an intimate view of Italy. And I got it all. I went to Mass 5 or 6 times during the trip and said my regular morning and evening prayers. The walk itself was full of spirituality, the effort, the sacrifice, nature, sunshine only proved the whole world is a church with God present everywhere."

John Gallagher, North Carolina, USA

"Obviously the trail is what is, and although we did have mostly excellent weather on our pilgrimage, that can't be changed either. Support from all the guides couldn't have been better. I'm not sure we got a complete picture of how challenging the way 'could' be, because our weather during the two weeks was very accommodating: it wasn't in general too hot, and very little rain fell on us during the walking portion of our days. I would say, though, that the people participating on the pilgrimages should be in excellent condition and have a certainty that they can walk a considerable distance over multiple days. Also, the possibility of blisters should be emphasized. Participants should be educated in best blister prevention techniques, and proper blister treatment products should be carried by all participants. [...] Combined with the cultural and spiritual components I think this pilgrimage is a first-rate experience. I would definitely recommend it to my spiritually-minded friends."

Gary Gregg, Seattle, USA

"Coming from a flat geographical area, the mountains were more than I expected. I am grateful you offered options to work around that or I might still be on the trail. The St. Francis Camino is not for the faint of heart. The mountains are difficult if you are in average shape or from a flat geographical environment. However, the trail is beautiful and restful until the suburbs of Rome, as not many pilgrims travel this route, and there are only a few places where one needs to be on major roads. ... It was so moving and unbelievable to pass through the Holy Doors and walk down St. Peter's aisle. I got goose bumps from the presence I felt there. I still am in awe wondering how this kid from a small town in Michigan got there. It was truly an amazing and highly spiritual trip for me that I will hold dear to my heart for as long as I live."

Jennifer Martin, Virginia, USA

"The humidity was not something I had prepared for, and it was challenging! You should be in really good shape before attempting this walk. There is a mountain every day, and each day ends with a mountain! There are far less people walking this way than the Camino, less stops during the day - it's more remote. Language can be an issue at times, the locals aren't as accustomed to seeing pilgrims, either."

Teresa Cardoni, Colorado, USA

RESOURCES

Books

- *The Way of Francis*, guidebook by Sandy Brown published by Cicerone.
- *On the Road with Saint Francis*, guidebook by Angela Seracchioli published by Terre di Mezzo.
- For more on the life of St. Francis, see *St. Francis of Assisi: Passion, Poverty and the Man who Transformed the Catholic Church*, by Bret Thoman, published by TAN Books, 2016.
- For more on the life of St. Clare, see *St. Clare of Assisi: Light from the Cloister*, by Bret Thoman, published by TAN Books, 2017.

Travel Agencies Specializing in the St. Francis Camino

http://www.stfrancispilgrimages.com/walking-caminos.html

www.ilmestierediviaggiare.it

Websites/Blogs on the St. Francis Camino:

Via di Francesco (Way of Francis) official Camino website
www.viadifrancesco.it/en/

St Francis Rieti Valley (*Italian only*)
www.camminodifrancesco.it

Sandy Brown's blog
https://caminoist.org/

ACKNOWLEDGEMENTS

It is said that a book is not written by a person, but by a community. This is certainly the case with this book, as it would not have been possible without the efforts of many of the people listed below. Their love for the Italian outdoors, the experience of Camino, and St. Francis is obvious to anyone who has met them or read their work.

Thanks, first of all, are due to all those individuals who worked tirelessly to pave the way for the St. Francis Camino. There were many (and I apologize in advance if I have omitted anyone).

To: Diego di Paolo, of Rieti, for his initiative in the *"Cammino di Francesco"* in Rieti (the trails connecting the four Franciscan sanctuaries), In collaboration with the Provincial government of Rieti and the Franciscans; Angela Seracchioli who wrote the pioneering guidebook, *"Di qui passò Francesco"* ("On the Road with Saint Francis"); Kees Roodenburg who published an early guidebook in German, *Franziskusweg*; Giordano Picchi who created the *"Cammino di Assisi"*.

To: Gianluigi Bettin of Sviluppumbria and Mons. Paolo Giulietti, former auxiliary bishop Perugia, the Basilica of St. Francis in Assisi, the dioceses of Umbria, the regional government of Umbria, numerous municipalities in Umbria, for their efforts creating the *Via di Francesco* ("Way of Francis").

To: Salvatore Accardi, founder of *Il Mestiere di Viaggiare* travel agency specializing in Italian Caminos, for his breadth of knowledge and experience of the trail and environs, in addition to his work familiarizing me with the St. Francis Camino.

To: Sandy Brown for preparing the way for English-speaking pilgrims with his English-language guidebook, *The Way of Francis* (Cicerone Press, 2015).

To: Alessandro Gullo, Umbrian and Assisi guide, for his unrivalled enthusiasm in guiding, his keen insight into Franciscan spirituality, and his gift for being able to draw participants into the pilgrimage experience as well as bring the pilgrimage into participants' lives.

To: Mons. Giulietti, current Archbishop of Lucca, for his guidance and for writing the Foreword to this book.

To: the readers of this manuscript: Jean Granier, Brenda Harris, Amy Bizzarri, Rho Densmore, and Bo Swanson.

Most of all, I would like to thank my family and my wife, Katia, for supporting and loving me in all my endeavors!

Lastly, this book is dedicated to all those who long to experience St. Francis of Assisi by walking in his footsteps in his native central Italy.

About the Author

Bret Thoman, OFS has been a member of the Secular Franciscan Order (Third Order of St. Francis) since 2003. He has a master's degree in Italian from Middlebury College, a BA from the University of Georgia in foreign languages, and a certificate in Franciscan Studies. Bret has written and published three books and translated numerous books from Italian to English. While working as an interpreter for CNN, he translated the papal conclave and announced the election of Pope Francis live. However, his main activity is organizing pilgrimages for St. Francis Pilgrimages, the company he founded in 2004. He is also an FAA-licensed pilot and has logged over 3,500 hours of flight time. He is partial to Latin, Gregorian chant and incense, and he spends his free time reading classics, hiking or biking anywhere not on asphalt. He currently lives in Loreto, Italy with his wife and three children.

Bret can be contacted at: bret.thoman@gmail.com
www.stfrancispilgrimages.com

Printed in Great Britain
by Amazon